"Talli Moellering's book *Let's Talk About S-E-X* provides a road map, in often uncharted territory, for parents to guide their teenage sons and daughters toward healthy sexual relationships in adulthood. In the sexualized culture our children live in, families need practical strategies for managing sexuality, dating, and relationships. This book shares a multitude of strategies and encourages parents to embrace the powerful role they have in shaping tween and teen sexual activity. The concepts presented throughout this book are simple, practical—yet eye-opening. Reading this book can have a positive effect on your family for generations to come."

— Dr. Doug Rosenau, psychologist, professor, certified sex therapist, best-selling author of *A Celebration of Sex* and *Dance of the Sexes*, and co-author of *Soul Virgins: Redefining Single Sexuality* and *Total Intimacy*

"I have the privilege of speaking to thousands of teenage girls each year, and Talli's book is right on target!! Teenagers today are so emotionally overwhelmed by the desensitized sexual culture...trying to process through their emotions requires an army of support. As parents we need the knowledge to provide the support they need. Talli's easy-to-read and no-nonsense approach empowers just that. My husband and I will be sharing these insights with our children —hope you will too."

— Leigh Cappillino, Point of Grace (Girls of Grace)

"Parents looking for a user-friendly guide to raising healthy teens will love this positive and practical book. Talli clearly outlines how to engage in sexual health conversations with your teen son or daughter, helping parents be directive and proactive—starting now. This book lives up to the promise to equip parents to counter the culture which threatens our future—today's teens."

— Kim Ketola, author of *Cradle My Heart: Finding God's Love After Abortion*

"Talli has been around the block professionally many times and knows her stuff when it comes to having her finger on the pulse of the sexualized culture of today's youth. If you have been entrusted with influencing the next generation—whether they are your own kids or someone else's—consider this book a solid resource for you to lean into and learn from."

— Michael Todd Wilson, licensed professional counselor, certified sex therapist, and co-author of *Soul Virgins: Redefining Single Sexuality*

"In my research with thousands of teens, I found that their most powerful influence is not peers but a great desire for freedom—and that "under the influence" of freedom, even good kids can make unhealthy choices. Since that especially applies to sex, and as the mom of a teen daughter myself, I am so grateful for Talli's practical experience and wisdom in this hypersexualized culture. Through her book, Talli shows us how to help our kids understand that freedom brings both choices and consequences and how to help them navigate their inevitable choices with maturity and thoughtfulness."

— Shaunti Feldhahn, social researcher and best-selling author of *For Women Only* and *For Parents Only*

"Talli Moellering is a highly engaging and down-to-earth speaker when it comes to addressing those sensitive topics that parents must, but are many times tentative to, discuss with their teens. Talli's main objective is to empower parents to talk to their teen about the hot topic of teen sex and related dangers. She uses a "whole person" approach which includes the physical, psychological, social, and financial connections to teen sexual activity. Her statistics and facts are compelling…her sense of urgency is palpable…and her discussion tips are frank, realistic, and practical. Parents walk away with much to think about, armed with a plethora of ideas for these frank discussions with their teens, and asking when Talli can come back and speak again!"

— Principal, Forsyth County Middle School, Georgia

"Every parent's dreaded nightmare is the day they have to have the sex talk. Talli Moellering provides invaluable resources for every parent who longs to prepare their child for the realities of this highly sexualized world but has no idea how to do it. Talli will give you both tools and insights into the critical issues and educate you about what and how to talk to your teen."

— Jennifer Stuckert, MA MFT, LPC

"Aaaah…words of truth, I agreed with Talli 100%. Now my mission is to implement her ideas! It's doable. God never promised it would be easy to parent but has promised He would never give me more than I can handle with Him by my side. Thank you for giving me the motivation to renew my commitment to open communication and listening more than I talk."

— Lynn, mother of three

"Talli has delivered on all counts: her book is a thoughtful, thorough, and highly readable resource for safely guiding our adolescent children through the obstacle course of growing up in a sex-saturated culture. This is a must read for every parent of a child under the age of 25!"

— Sandy Christiansen, MD, FACOG, Medical Director of the Care Net Pregnancy Center of Frederick in Maryland

"I thoroughly enjoyed reading the book. It's a great tool for families to have when they're raising their teenage sons and daughters. I can honestly say it is the best book I have ever read on this subject. I especially appreciate how it combines the medical, physical, and even the spiritual components of this topic. Thank you for creating this amazing resource to equip and protect the young people growing up in today's sexualized society."

— Dr. Chip Harbaugh, Board Certified Pediatrician, previous CEO and Chairman of the Board of Kids Health First Pediatric Alliance, served on 5 national American Academy of Pediatrics committees plus the Center for Disease Control

"As the father of two girls and the uncle of nine nieces, I need all the help I can get. Talli's book is a must read! I wish my wife and I had been able to read it years ago. It would have helped us navigate those very necessary, but oh so awkward, conversations with our daughters. Talli has a great style. She is direct and easy to understand, while never shaming or judging. You owe it to yourselves and your children to read *Let's Talk About S-E-X*. It will help equip you to be the best parent you can be."

— Jeff Foxworthy, comedian

"I want to thank you again for speaking at our school. It was a great talk that opened the eyes of the parents in attendance. As a few of the parents arrived, they told me they had to leave early, however, I noticed they stayed until you finished. Everyone was totally engrossed in your presentation. Although sex is an uncomfortable subject for parents to comprehend in the context of their own children, you provided them with valuable insight that will help them deal with those situations that do arise as well as what to say to their kids to avoid problems before they become reality. You are an excellent speaker and give a wonderful presentation!"

— Beth, middle school PTA president

LET'S TALK ABOUT
S~E~X

Equipping Parents to Tackle Sex and Dating with
Truth and Tenacity

TALLI MOELLERING

14.99

LET'S TALK ABOUT S-E-X
Talli Moellering
Copyright © 2015 by Talli Moellering

Published by TLC Consultants, Inc. Atlanta, Georgia

For more information about this book or to contact the author, visit
http://www.tlcconsultantsinc.com/
Print ISBN 978-0-9861784-0-5
Electronic ISBN 978-0-9861784-1-2

Printed in the United States of America

The author has made every effort to ensure the accuracy of the information within this book was correct at time of publication. Some names and identifying details have been changed to protect the privacy of individuals.

The author does not assume and hereby disclaims any liability to any party for any loss, damage, or disruption caused by errors or omissions, whether such errors or omissions result from accident, negligence, or any other cause. This book is not intended as a substitute for the medical advice of physicians.

Cover design by Tiger Bright Studios

Contents

For

David: My best friend and the love of my life. Although I know the truth, that you pursued me, I'm willing to admit that I would have pursued you, had you given me the chance. You are, and always have been, better than I deserve.

Maddison, Brittyn, Jordyn: My blessings and my teachers. I'm fully aware that having a mom who is known as "the sex lady" has placed you in several unique conversations. Thank you for courageously handling the awkward pause. You are each beautiful on the inside and out. I can't wait to see what is yet to come. As always, value yourself, set the bar high, and guard your heart!

Mom: My steadfast prayer warrior. What an honor it is to know that each day you choose to quietly yet boldly pray over me, my family, and my work. The hedge of protection that you have placed around our family is more than evident, and we are forever grateful.

Dad: My cheerleader. Not a day has passed in my entire life when I have questioned how much you love me. I know I'm your favorite, but don't worry, I won't tell my sisters. Thanks for letting me be the "Talli of the Tal." It's an honor!

Judy: The instigator. You prayed. You poked. You prodded. You pushed. There are Judy tones and talks throughout this book. I wish I would have gotten it done in time to place it in your hands, but no need to worry, we will celebrate together in due time.

INTRODUCTION

Not too long ago, I met Daphne, a middle-class, actively engaged mom of three teenagers. This is her story:

My oldest daughter was spending all of her time in bed, depressed and bad tempered. I couldn't feel a temperature or see any other symptoms, but she was adamant that it was the flu. She stated she didn't feel well and wanted to be left alone. Her room was dark, and the only time she ventured out was to use the bathroom.

After the third day, I scheduled a doctor's appointment. He acted a little odd, but he diagnosed her with the flu—a virus that would eventually go away. I believed him and really wasn't worried. I now look back and realize how naive I was.

It was only after she lay in her dark room for nearly a week, with no visible symptoms, that I began to question the situation. I started to challenge her, demanding to know what was going on. We ended up yelling about mundane, irrelevant issues until she broke down in tears. I started to feel fearful and asked if this had anything to do with the boy she was dating. She nodded. I swallowed.

"Did you have sex with him?"

She started crying even harder but eventually said yes.

I felt nauseous. "Are you pregnant?"

She looked straight at me, tears rolling down her sweet face. "What do you think?" She collapsed on her bed, crying so hard she was gasping.

I felt numb, totally numb. I couldn't feel anything. Here I was, excited that my daughter was getting ready to graduate from high school, and she was telling me I was about to be a grandmother. I left the room in a daze and locked myself in my own room. I could hear her wails but could not bring myself to comfort her. I actually felt like I had been told that someone I loved had just died. I now understand there had been a death—the death of my daughter's innocence.

I had no idea that she was having sex. The guy she was dating seemed nice—a little cocky, but nice. Was I really that out of touch? This was the daughter who still had to be told to clean up her room, who panicked when she got a bad grade, who didn't know how to cook or do laundry.

A few hours later—which felt like an eternity—I was interrupted by a knock on the door. My fragile daughter entered, sat next to me, and said, "I'm so sorry, Mom. I'm sorry. Please say something. I'm so sorry." She just kept crying and saying it over and over. She was frightened and vulnerable, but I couldn't think of what to say.

I meet moms like Daphne often. They bring their daughters to the women's clinic that I lead. They approach me after I teach a parents' sexual health workshop in a local school. They find me in church or at my youngest daughter's volleyball games. They share their stories, their questions, and their fears. They're lost in the sex-filled, always-connected culture where their tweens and teens are growing up. Like Daphne, most parents often have no idea what to say.

I don't know what your childhood was like, but when I was a teenager in a small town in the Midwest, the world seemed simpler and safer. Sure, puberty meant oily skin and acne, roller-coaster moods that swung from angst to exuberance to depression to aggression. A voracious appetite, or no appetite at all. An awkward body growing in unexpected places and leaking at unexpected times. The first fluttering of mysterious, magnetic attractions toward others. We experienced the draw of "young love"— relationships and romance, sexual interests, and perhaps even seduction. We saw public displays of affection. But there wasn't graphic sex everywhere we looked—on cable, in movies, in advertisements, and even on our phones. We weren't talking about rainbow parties and sexting. We'd never heard of the Internet, let alone Internet porn.

Looking back, I recognize that many of the teens around me were having sex. The numbers show that more teens were sexually active in the 1980s and '90s than they are today.[1] But it was all happening behind closed doors, while the adults in our lives looked awkwardly the other way. I remember boys getting caught with dirty magazines (that they took from their fathers), whispered stories of wild exploits on spring break adventures, and the darker rumor that a girl was out of school for a week because she had an abortion. But S-E-X? We all pretended it wasn't happening.

A few decades later, here we are, parents of preteens or teens ourselves. The dynamics of puberty—the acne and mood swings and awkward growth spurts—are pretty much the same, but they're happening earlier than ever before. A century ago, girls, on average, were 14.6 years old when they reached puberty; it's 10.5 now.[2] The first signs of puberty in many girls now appear more than a year earlier than they did a generation ago, and more than twice as many girls are showing signs of very early puberty—even before age eight.[3]

Our kids are quite literally growing up faster than ever—and they're not nearly as naive about sexuality as I was. This is one of the first generations to navigate global digital domains as adolescents; they're pioneers in a radically connected world that presents more temptations, looser morals, fewer consequences—and even crimes—related to teen sexuality than we could ever have anticipated. On a daily basis, teens are exposed to television shows using sex to draw viewers, commercials advertising sex to sell products, Hollywood glamorizing sex, parents tolerating sex, the digital world basically showing them sex, and places of worship ignoring sex.

Sociology professor Tony Campolo says, "I am convinced we don't live in a generation of bad kids. We live in a generation of kids who know too much too soon."[4]

We've heard the stories:

- The fifteen-year-old girl who drank until she passed out at a party and was assaulted sexually by a group of boys who took photos of the incident and then passed them around school. She committed suicide eight days later.[5]

- The teachers (both men and women, in almost every US state) caught sending and receiving sexually suggestive or nude photos with their students.

- An urban myth about a "teen pregnancy pact," in which a half-dozen girls in the same high school agreed to get pregnant so that they could raise their babies together, seeming totally plausible in a world where reality TV shows like *16 and Pregnant*, *Teen Mom*, and *Teen Mom 2* make instant celebrities out of sexually active high school students.

These events might seem foreign, accounts and stories from somewhere out there, involving people we don't know. But something similar is happening closer than you think. Exposure to sexual behavior happens to tweens and teens everywhere, regardless of your neighborhood, faith, income, or race.

How would you feel if the faces of those stories hit closer to home? Or even *in your home*?

IT COULD NEVER HAPPEN TO MY KID

Are you sure? One-third of all teens report that they have had sex by their sixteenth birthday. By the time they're nineteen, that number jumps to seven in ten. A quarter of teens admit to "sexting" sexually explicit messages or photos. Two thousand teen girls get pregnant in the United States every day. And teens are at heightened risk for sexually transmitted infections.[6]

And in case you think your son or daughter is the exception to this, those statistics aren't drawn just from "rough" or "bad" public schools. Teens from privileged neighborhoods, private schools, and Parochial schools are also experimenting with sexual activity at younger ages. One health teacher shared with me, "I teach at a Christian school with kids from conservative homes. What parents don't realize is that these kids are sexually active too. The teens here seem to refrain from sexual intercourse, but they do everything else and then talk about their virginity status."

In the heat of passion, even the "smartest" teenagers don't always think about the ramifications of a decision to become sexually active. Couple that with their desperate search for approval from peers and the incredible social pressures connected to teen relationships, and we have an age-old recipe for unhealthy decision making.

I've counseled hundreds of teen couples who are facing unexpected pregnancies, and I've taught thousands of teens about the fundamentals of making healthy sexual choices. I've listened to their questions and their stories. And it's taught me this: you, parents, are the most important influence standing between your teen and the pressures of a hyper-sexed culture. Not their teachers, not their youth group leaders, and certainly not their friends. You are the best person to help your daughter or son move toward the best, healthiest physical and relational behavior.

HOW DID A MOM LIKE ME START TALKING ABOUT THINGS LIKE THIS?

I didn't expect to become an educator and expert in teen sexuality.

I grew up in a loving, close-knit, conservative Christian home. I went to a private Christian school through eighth grade. To say I was sheltered in my younger years would be an understatement. But when I was fourteen years old, my dad's job relocated us to a new state, I started going to a large public school, and my oldest sister announced that she was pregnant. It all happened within one year. Needless to say, the changes confused me and, for a time, shook our family to the core.

I vividly remember the day Kelli came home from her freshman year of college, two months pregnant and already starting to show. I thought something seemed odd when she got out of her car, but being young and naive, I didn't understand the long, awkward pause in the family room after she shared the news with our parents. I remember silence, emotion, and a few questions. Before he excused himself to his bedroom, my dad gently shared, "God doesn't make mistakes." My mom followed him and closed the door behind them. Kelli was in a season of rebellion, so my parents were not necessarily shocked, but they were obviously concerned and, rightfully so, disappointed about the unplanned "situation."

We were a Christian family. Kelli was raised in a Christian home. She graduated from a Christian high school. She was attending a Christian college. She obviously wasn't married. She definitely wasn't "supposed" to be having sex. And we, as a family, were not prepared to experience a crisis pregnancy. But still, the idea of a baby sounded kind of cute and fun to me.

Within three weeks, Kelli did what Christian girls who got pregnant back then did; she married the baby's father. A few months later she gave birth to my oldest nephew, an adorable bundle of joy who quickly melted our family's hearts and started to dissolve the heartbreak and confusion of an unplanned pregnancy.

A few years later, I found myself, now a college freshman, in a Public Speaking 101 class. We were assigned to give a debate speech on a topic from a list provided by the professor. Based on my family's experience and the season of life I was in personally, struggling with temptations and boundaries, I decided to select "saving sex for marriage" as my topic.

When it was my turn to deliver my speech in front of the class, I started off strong, sharing my research pertaining to sex being created for marriage and the importance of babies being born into a home with two parents. But by the end of the speech, I was tearing up as I emotionally divulged my family's story. I embarrassed myself and probably made my classmates uncomfortable. Little did I know at the time, but I had personal, unfinished business that needed to be addressed.

Thankfully, my professor was moved by my raw emotion and passion for the topic, and he gave me a decent grade, which I probably didn't deserve. (It probably also helped that I was in a Christian college, where abstinence—the word often connected to this topic and a word I've come to dislike—was not only encouraged but required.) I didn't realize it then, but that speech was the first of thousands that I would give on the subject of teen sexuality.

Around the same time, my tennis doubles partner (yes, I played tennis in college) introduced me to one of the star football players on campus. I thought he was really cute and—whether he wants to admit it or not—he thought I was pretty hot. David was a few years older than me, but we started dating and experienced the fairy tale relationship that you hardly ever hear about now. We fell head over heels in love, got engaged, and married.

After the wedding, I moved to my husband's hometown, in northern Indiana. He went to work for the family company, while I worked full time, settled into my new wife duties, and met people within the community. During this transitional time, my in-laws were actively involved in the start-up of a crisis pregnancy center—often referred to as a CPC—and I started volunteering with them. I was eager to help families experiencing what our family had experienced a few years earlier.

I remember thinking there was an obvious solution to unplanned pregnancies, and all we needed to do was share it with the clients—just don't have sex unless you are married. It seemed simple to me, until I met the real women—single, married, young, and old—who were processing through their dilemmas of crisis pregnancy.

These experiences led me to really dig into understanding what it was about unplanned pregnancy that really broke my heart. What made me lay awake at night? Which patient cases tugged so deeply at my heart that I couldn't just walk away? The answer, every time, were the teenagers. I distinctly remember looking at the director of the CPC on a Thursday night in 1991 and saying, "I want to talk to these teen girls *before* they walk in our door. I want to eliminate their need for our services." She smiled and said, "Talli, I think you just found your calling!"

Since those days, I've taught sexual health to over forty thousand students. I've trained thousands of health teachers to implement their sex education curriculum in the classroom. I've presented the message of Pure Sexual Freedom to a multitude of parents. I direct two women's clinics (previously known as CPCs), and, most importantly, I am still married to the man of my dreams and am the mother of three precious girls who are now teenagers and young adults. Every one of those experiences has changed who I am as a person and how I function daily as a woman, a wife, a mother, and a friend.

Through these roles, I've heard stories of every kind. I met the young girl who was raped and doesn't know who did it, the daughter with a positive pregnancy test whose parents tell her she's on her own. I've stood next to a couple as they see their baby on an ultrasound screen and cry because this wasn't part of their plan. I've celebrated with the teen mom who didn't think she could go through with the pregnancy as she holds her baby boy in her arms. I have dug deeply into the national resources and research. I have presented sexual health in both public and private schools.

In all of these settings—whether it be a counseling room, the classroom, or a parent gathering—I realized parents are not tackling the constantly evolving reality of teen sexual activity, and it's time to start doing so.

YOU'RE NOT ALONE

However old your child is now, and whether you have sons or daughters, the next few years may seem scary. But don't worry. You're not in this alone. The Pure Sexual Freedom model, which we'll explore in the following chapters, is designed to give parents a practical map to guide you through some of the really tough sexual health topics with your teens.

I wrote this book to equip parents of tweens and teens to calmly yet confidently have conversations with their teens about sexual activity. My main goals for this material are to:

- Explain, in evidence-based terms, how not engaging in at-risk sexual activity during the teen years is the healthiest choice for your teen both physically and emotionally.

- Inform you of current, important facts pertaining to teen sex and dating.

- Remove barriers that keep you from discussing the importance of healthy sexual boundaries, self-respect, and respect for others.

- Equip you with relevant, creative concepts and tools related to these topics.

Throughout the book, I will share relevant research, statistics, and cultural trends, as well as stories from teens, parents, and teachers. Hopefully, the frank snapshots will encourage you to be proactive in your parenting and compassionate to families who are struggling with these issues. The ideas or concepts covered here can be considered controversial. We will address many of the controversies in these chapters. Throughout our time together, you might feel as though I'm being rather blunt—I hear that a lot. Please understand that there is simply not a soft, comfy way to discuss some of these issues. I want you to have facts and statistics. It's time to say it like it is. We need honesty and candor in a conversation as serious as this, for the sake and safety of our kids—and maybe even for generations to follow.

It may be hard to see now, but as we guide our teens through the minefield of sexual temptation and changing cultural mores, we can be confident that someday, probably a little later in life, they will appreciate that we had enough courage to do so.

PART 1: YOUR KIDS NEED YOU

Jeff and Allison had no reason to suspect that anything was wrong. Their fourteen-year-old, Taylor, was an athletic kid with good grades. He'd been close to the same group of friends since elementary school. He played on two sports teams, including the state-wide traveling baseball team, which kept him busy after school and many weekends. When he was home, he played video games and chatted online with his teammates and school friends almost constantly. His parents had never heard him express an interest in girls, although they'd noticed that some of his friends now had "girlfriends" who, as far as they could tell, the boys only saw at school. Allison asked Taylor if he had a girlfriend at school, and he said no. She let it drop, thinking he was too young for all of that anyway.

So Taylor's parents were completely unprepared when Jeff got a call one afternoon from the police. They'd picked up Taylor and a teenage girl hanging out behind the mall. When Jeff met a mortified Taylor at the police station, the story came out. He'd met a girl from a rival high school at a baseball tournament the month before, and they'd been texting and chatting online every day since. When Jeff looked at Taylor's phone, he was shocked to see that the girl had sent his son revealing photos of herself…and that his son had responded with words that even made Jeff blush. After several weeks of back-and-forth graphic messages, and repeated requests from the girl, the teens had devised a plan to cut school and spend the day together.

Allison and Jeff were stunned. Their son had risked suspension and his place on the baseball team for a girl that they didn't even know existed!

11

1

MOM, DAD, I HAVE A QUESTION...

PARENTHOOD. What a responsibility...and what joy! We teach our children to walk and talk, tie their shoes, throw a ball, ride a bike, recite ABCs, and read. As they grow, we teach them to swing a bat, drive a car, handle money, cultivate positive friendships, and value themselves.

We're there for monumental milestones: the first day of school, first recital, first ball game, prom, graduation. We're there to teach them patiently, love them abundantly, and do all we can daily to grow our children into kind and responsible adults. We want our sons and daughters to experience happy, healthy, and fruitful lives with minimal difficulties and pain.

Yet when it comes to something as frightfully important and life changing as their sexual health, there seems to be an innate disconnect between parents and their tweens and teens. The parents who attend my workshops often assume that their teens are going to learn about sex somewhere, somehow, or from someone else. I hear a lot of:

> *He's too young to be thinking about sex.*
>
> *If I bring it up, he will start thinking about it.*
>
> *I don't know the right things to say.*
>
> *I don't want to embarrass her.*
>
> *What if she asks me about my own sexual past?*

My teen doesn't listen to anything I say.

My teen probably knows more about dating and sex today than I do.

Whether it's because they feel unprepared or ashamed, parents end up abdicating what may be the most important part of their teen's transition to adulthood to teachers, doctors, and youth group leaders—and, more disturbingly, to their peers and the media. They stand by silently, fearfully hold their breath, and hope their teens will come out of this hormonally driven stage of life intact.

In today's sex-driven climate, our teens will learn about sex; it is going to happen. But will the outcome be the one we hoped for? From a parental perspective, it takes far more than hope, prayers, and good wishes to guarantee our teens will end up on the healthy side of this topic.

WHAT YOUR TEEN ALREADY KNOWS

The realization that our young, sweet, innocent sons and daughters will become sexual beings with minds and desires of their own, and that this will happen while they're living in our homes, can be a difficult thing to grasp, let alone accept. How can a kid who still needs you to sign a permission slip before he goes on a field trip be capable of thinking about—let alone experimenting with—sex?

Yet that's the reality. Tweens and teens know far more about sex than we might think. They hear about sex everywhere. Almost every popular TV show or movie targeted at teens incorporates some depiction of sex outside of marriage, but rarely does it explore the consequences. Then there are sidebar ads on "safe" websites. Sex in the news. Sex-fueled fashion. The 24/7 media culture idealizes celebrities who draw attention to themselves with shocking or outrageous behavior.

We've culturally become casual about sexual innuendos and stereotypes, and our kids are hearing about oral sex, hooking up, multiple partners, and "friends with benefits" years before they're ready for it. For the past few years, I've asked my ninth-grade classes to raise their hands if they'd seen the R-rated movie *Friends with Benefits*. Consistently, about 90% of them reported they had seen the movie, which ironically was nominated for a Teen Choice Award, even though most teenagers wouldn't be legally allowed into a theater to watch it.

Perhaps motivated or inspired by the sexually casual characters they see on TV, teens are no longer shy or reserved when it comes to showing their intentions. And since girls, generally speaking, mature faster and enter puberty earlier than boys, more and more they're becoming the early instigators. We've moved past the days of "girls don't call boys"— and in fact, many parents report that in middle school and early high school, teens have swung to the opposite extreme. Parents who thought that their biggest challenge would be protecting their daughters from the stereotype of hormone-driven boys are finding that their bigger challenges come from sheltering their young teen sons from girls who text "can U sneak out 2nite."[7]

Regardless of the cultural changes, two constants remain among the tween and teen population: curiosity and hormones. As puberty arrives and hormones ramp up, it's natural and normal for a "tweenager" (ten-, eleven-, or twelve-year-old) to be curious about relationships. Whether parents realize it or not, research shows that the typical average American tween is at least intrigued with the idea of kissing someone. They are aware of it, thinking about it, and probably even surrounded by a few kids who have been confident enough to give it a try—if they're not actually trying it out themselves.

This does not mean every tween is kissing or that a tween who has never thought about kissing is abnormal. All young people develop at different rates. But thanks to the public displays of affection we are all exposed to, it's probably safe to assume that your daughter or son, regardless of age, is exploring some kind of sexual thoughts and questions.

Their curiosity doesn't stop with kissing. Several of the sexual health classes I teach are in middle schools, for students who are generally between thirteen and fourteen years old. At the end of the teaching session, I invite any student who has a question to write it on an index card and drop it into a box at the back of the room. They don't put their name on the card, to ensure their privacy.

Here are some questions I've heard over and over, in their own words:

What if you lie and tell one of your friends you had sex so they'll think you're cool, and then they tell everyone else?

Can you still get your period when you are pregnant?

When can I start dating?

I've played around with sexual activity but didn't have intercourse. Should I get tested for an infection?

I really want to go out with this guy, but all he talks about is sex. How can I go out with him and not do it?

If you have warts on your penis and you get them treated, can you still pass the infection to someone else?

If you masturbate then stick your fingers in a girl, can she get pregnant?

Why do my parents act so weird whenever they talk about sex?

How can I get guys to notice me?

Why does everyone act like it is only the guys pressuring the girls to have sex?

Is it okay for us to live together first before we get married? If not, then what if we wait until we're married and then find out the sex isn't any good?

Can I have oral sex and still say I'm a virgin?

If I'm gay, there's no risk that my boyfriend and I can get pregnant. Why shouldn't we hook up?

"Hooking up" is easier than having a relationship, so why not hook up?

If my partner and I make it official, am I allowed to talk to other guys?

If you're just going out, is it okay to make out with another guy?

These are the types of questions that our teens are pondering. For some parents, these questions are a concern. To others, these questions are no big deal. Regardless of whether you're surprised or worried, here's the catch: curiosity almost always leads to action.

By fifteen, 30% of teens will have had sexual intercourse. And by nineteen, 70% will.[8] A lot seems to change between natural sixth-grade curiosity and high school graduation.

It's sobering, and scary. We love our kids. We're aware of the difficult ramifications connected to such trends, and we're trying to teach them how to thrive in the midst of this ever-changing culture.

In light of the questions above, I think a companion list is in order. Parents, what are your thoughts?

- Does this list of questions surprise you in any way?

- How would you respond to these questions?

- Are you prepared to talk to your son or daughter about teen sexual activity?

- Have you prepared your teen to counter the peer pressure to have sex?

- Are you ready to intervene when your son or daughter begins to make choices related to sex?

- Have you considered that having a proactive parent might be the primary reason a teen chooses not to engage in at-risk sexual activity?

WHAT YOUR TEEN NEEDS

In the classroom, I review the students' question cards and answer as many as I can, but then I also challenge them to go home and talk with their parent(s) about these topics. More often than not, the students will roll their eyes as if to say, "You have got to be kidding me!"

My challenge to you is similar: **Talk with your tweens and teens about these topics.** Teens (yours included) have these kinds of questions, and it's time to ready yourself and provide them with the answers. In doing so, you have an opportunity to mold their values and perspective in the area of sexuality.

The idea of sex is alluring to still-developing minds. But, as we can see in the questions they ask, it's also confusing. The teens and tweens I meet are full of insecurities and uncertainties, as well as misinformation and mistakes. They're getting conflicting messages from the culture and from their own developing bodies. They're making huge decisions. And whether they show it or not, they WANT you to be involved.

Your teenagers need you now more than ever. These are the times when we need to be the most diligent, present, and actively communicating with our teens, even if it's unpopular, uncomfortable, and (let's be honest) tiring.

During this precarious time, our teens need factual information, guideposts, and warning signs to help them navigate successfully. They need your help processing through the ideas and misconceptions that they pick up from their friends and the media. They need to be lovingly, honestly educated about potential consequences of their actions; they need to hear that "it won't happen to me" is an unrealistic belief and not a valid reason to be sexually active.

They need to hear it from their mom and/or dad. And they need to hear it even when you don't think they're listening.

There's a lot at stake here. How your teen handles the temptations and pressures of sex over the next few years will determine parts of their future in ways that are easily recognizable—broken hearts, teen pregnancy, sexually transmitted infections (STIs)—and in ways that are more subtle, such as dysfunctional behaviors, addictions, post-abortion symptoms and lifelong relationship issues. The innocence of the teen years has been washed away by the tide of our unbridled, oversexed culture, leading young people to believe the propaganda that teen sexual activity is just a normal part of growing up and is consequence-free.

Teenagers need their parents to be courageous and share the facts. They want straight, truthful answers! They want to know what you think:

- How far is too far?

- Do you think it's okay for teens to have sex?

- Do you think it's possible for teens to say no to sex?

- Will using a condom or another form of birth control protect them?

- Is hooking up really a big deal?

So get ready. The old one-time talk about the "birds and the bees" doesn't adequately cover the true ramifications of teen sexual activity. **Your teen *will* make a decision about sex.** Consider the consequences of *not* discussing it.

The best protection against the physical consequences and the heartache connected to teen sexual activity is to break our silence, set expectations, and talk about sexual health, our values, and our hopes for our teen's future. A positive and constructive approach to this topic sets the stage for developing open and ongoing dialogue.

Conversations with your teen regarding sexual activity cannot always be planned. Training them on this topic begins at birth and continues until you hear them say "I do" at their wedding. Often the best life lessons are learned in the midst of unscripted, teachable moments that present themselves during everyday living—when watching TV, or when your teen casually mentions something that's happening at school, or when you're shopping together for clothes and have to wade through all of the suggestive clothing...those are the moments when your teen will learn from your responses.

It takes courage to go against what society says is inevitable and set higher standards for our teens. It also takes a great amount of energy and intentional involvement in their lives. It's easier (in terms of effort) to give in and let the media messages raise our teens, but the outcome will be scary if we give in to this pattern of living. Don't give in! Fight for what is most valuable to you—actually, for **who** is most valuable to you. Teens often don't want you to know it, but you do have a huge impact on the choices they make. So go for it. Begin the conversation today.

2

WHO, ME? YOUR ROLE AS A PARENT

Y our teen will make a decision about sex. Will it be the decision you want them to make? Have you thought through the details of what that decision should look like?

Before you can guide your daughter or son through these conversations, you need to have thought through where you, personally, stand. In today's culture, there are widely different opinions pertaining to this topic, and every parent has their own personal sexual history, perspective, and beliefs that impact how they parent.

The following questions will help you start to see what your beliefs look like in practice.

1. How will I present information about sex to my son or daughter? (check all that apply)

   ☐ Hand them a book when their body starts to change.

   ☐ Hand them birth control before they go on their first date and make sure they know how to use it.

   ☐ Let them take the lead. I'll tell them I'm open to discussing this topic and to let me know if they have any questions, then let them tell me when they're ready.

   ☐ Let the health teachers at the school take care of it. They're the experts.

☐ When I decide my child is old enough to date, we will have a frank conversation about what my expectations are for their behavior.

☐ Incorporate conversations about healthy relationships and sexual health into our everyday life, keeping the topic open for discussion whenever needed and revisiting it often as my child continues to develop and mature.

☐ Other:

2. What do I believe is the purpose for sex? (check all that apply)

☐ Physical pleasure

☐ Intimate bonding between two people

☐ Procreation

☐ Emotional fulfillment

3. When was the last time I talked to my tween or teen about sex?

☐ I've never talked to my child about sex.

☐ When we had the "birds and bees" talk at the beginning of puberty.

☐ Within the past few weeks, when our conversation naturally ended up there because of something they saw/thought/heard.

☐ Recently, when they started asking questions and I didn't know what to say. (Why do you think I'm reading this book?)

☐ Other:

4. When was the last time I talked to my tween or teen about their personal boundaries in relationships?

☐ I'm waiting until they are old enough to date to talk to them about that.

☐ When I laid out the rules about dating, I explained what their boundaries needed to be.

☐ I've never talked to them about their boundaries.

☐ Within the past few weeks, when our conversation naturally ended up there because of something they saw/thought/heard.

☐ Other:

5. Have I thought through the dating guidelines for our children?

☐ Yes

☐ No

☐ Never thought about it

☐ I have, but we haven't talked to them about it yet.

6. What level(s) of physical contact do I believe is appropriate for teenagers? (check all that apply)

☐ Hugging

☐ Holding hands

☐ A kiss on the cheek

☐ Kissing on the lips

☐ "Making out" with clothes on

☐ "Making out" and touching parts of the body normally covered by underwear

☐ Technical virginity (a.k.a. "everything but" vaginal intercourse)

☐ Sexual intercourse

☐ It depends on the teenager's maturity level and relationship status.

☐ Other:

7. What level(s) of physical contact do I believe is appropriate only within marriage? (check all that apply)

☐ Hugging

☐ Holding hands

☐ A kiss on the cheek

☐ Kissing on the lips

☐ "Making out" with clothes on

☐ "Making out" and touching parts of the body normally covered by underwear

☐ Technical virginity (a.k.a. "everything but" vaginal intercourse)

☐ Sexual intercourse

☐ I don't think it's necessary to limit to marriage any sexual activity between consenting adults.

☐ Other:

8. What is my personal definition of "having sex"?

☐ Sexual intercourse (which means vaginal penetration)

☐ Sexual intercourse (which means vaginal, oral, and anal sex)

☐ Sexual activity in the "the underwear zone"

☐ Heavy kissing with the hands and the body involved

☐ Other:

9. How should acceptable boundaries for my teen's sexual activity be set?

☐ As the parent, I set the boundaries because teenagers aren't mature enough to know where to draw their own lines.

☐ My teen can and should make their own decisions, independent of pressure or my opinions; they need to take responsibility for their own behavior.

☐ I should educate my teen and let them know what I believe appropriate physical and emotional boundaries are, but then allow them to do what's best for them; I'll support them in whatever they choose.

    ☐ I should educate my teen, work with them to set boundaries that are appropriate, and then partner with them for accountability.

    ☐ Other:

10. What do I want my teen to believe about saving sex for marriage?

    ☐ Saving sex for marriage is both healthy and possible, and it makes sex within marriage better.

    ☐ Saving sex for marriage is a great idea, but with the average age of marriage rising, it's not really possible anymore.

    ☐ Women should be virgins on their wedding day to preserve their reputations, but it's not reasonable to expect that from men—"boys will be boys," after all.

    ☐ A person should experiment sexually when they're young so that they have enough experience to know who they want to settle down with.

    ☐ Other:

11. What do I personally believe about sex within the context of marriage?

    ☐ Sex is rarely a part of marriage.

    ☐ Sex within marriage can get stale, but that's the cost of having a long-term relationship.

    ☐ Sex in marriage is great, and it's fulfilling to grow sexually with one partner.

    ☐ Other:

12. How do I define sexual responsibility?

    ☐ Refraining from sexual intercourse until marriage

    ☐ Refraining from intimate sexual activity and sexual intercourse until marriage

    ☐ Refraining from sexual activity unless it's in a relationship defined by love

☐ Refraining from sexual activity until both people are adults and can make responsible decisions

☐ Refraining from sexual activity unless there is a mutual understanding of each person's monogamous commitment

☐ Other:

13. What influences do I believe my teen might struggle with/is struggling with? (check all that apply)

☐ Peer pressure

☐ Alcohol

☐ Drugs

☐ Media and social networking addiction

☐ Feelings of body insecurity

☐ Feelings of emotional insecurity and consuming desires for affection, affirmation, and acceptance

☐ Hormones and temptation to experiment sexually

☐ Adults and other older role models who are absent or demonstrate unhealthy relationships

☐ Other:

14. Have I intentionally created a safe place in our home, free from peer and media pressure, for my tween or teen to hang out and include their friends?

☐ Yes

☐ No

☐ Never even thought about it

☐ In some ways, but not totally

☐ Other:

15. Have I identified the areas at our house where my tween or teen might be tempted to engage in sexual activity (basement family room, private corners of the backyard, etc.)?

☐ Yes

☐ No

☐ Never even thought about it

☐ In some ways, but not totally

☐ Other:

16. Do I know the families of my child's friends, and do I know what their guidelines and priorities are?

   ☐ Yes, I know the parents of all their friends; before my son or daughter is allowed to go to anyone's house I must be comfortable with their family's values and decision making.

   ☐ Yes, I'm friendly with the parents of all their friends and have talked with them about our house guidelines and expectations.

   ☐ Yes, I'm friendly with many of the families of their friends, but I've never explicitly talked to them about how they raise their children; that seems rude or invasive.

   ☐ I've met some of their friends but don't know their families.

   ☐ No, I don't know much about who they hang out with or what their friends' home lives are like.

   ☐ Other:

17. If my teen could copy my past dating experiences, would I want them to do so?

   ☐ Yes

   ☐ No, but I don't want them to know it.

   ☐ No, but I have processed through how to use my past to help my teen make healthier choices.

18. I believe the purpose of dating should be: (check all that apply)

   ☐ To have fun

   ☐ To get to know another person better

☐ To learn more about yourself

☐ To flirt and explore your sexual identity

☐ To consider what type of person you want to marry someday

☐ There is no purpose; it's just what young people do.

☐ Other:

19. Have I discussed the purpose of dating with my teen?

☐ Yes

☐ No

☐ Never really thought about it

20. At what age is/was my teen allowed to date?

☐ 13

☐ 14

☐ 15

☐ 16

☐ 17

☐ 18

☐ There is no set age; it depends on their personal maturity and responsibility.

☐ Other:

21. Listed below are some common dating guidelines. Check the guidelines you think are appropriate for your home and family.

☐ My teen will be allowed to date when they are _____ years old.

☐ Dating is a privilege, not a right assigned by age. We'll decide when our child is old enough to date based on their maturity and behavior, not their age.

☐ My teen must introduce me to anyone they would like to start dating and arrange a time for me to meet the individual.

- ☐ My teen must provide me with a phone number for the parent(s) of anyone they want to date and understand that I will call and introduce myself before they are allowed to go out alone together.

- ☐ My teen is not allowed to be alone in a house with their date.

- ☐ My teen is not allowed to be in bedrooms with their date, even if other people are there.

- ☐ While hanging out at our house, if they are alone in any room, the door must be open.

- ☐ My teen has a curfew and is expected to honor it. This includes how late their date is allowed to stay at our home.

- ☐ My teen has a social media curfew and is expected to honor it. This means no Facebook, Twitter, texting, or phone calls after a certain hour.

- ☐ My teen can only go out in groups; one-on-one dating is not permitted.

- ☐ My teen knows what an "emergency situation" is and what to do in case it happens.

- ☐ My teen must tell me where they are going on their date. If plans change, they must check in with me before they transfer to another location.

- ☐ I expect my teen to be picked up at our front door/to go to their date's front door to meet them, rather than sending a text and waiting outside in his car.

- ☐ My teen isn't allowed to be alone in a car with their date.

- ☐ If my teen is spending the night at a friend's, they must call me when they arrive and are in for the night, preferably from a landline. If there is no landline, if I have any doubts about their location, it is their responsibility to find some way to reassure me (putting the friend's parent on the phone, texting a photo, etc.).

- ☐ All dating privileges will be revoked if I discover provocative photos or online posts that my teen has sent or received.

☐ "Missionary dating" (dating someone who doesn't share my teen's values or faith but who "needs help" and can be "changed") is not permitted. My teen is only allowed to date other teens who share similar goals and morals.

☐ We may permit "missionary dating" if we have met and like the date, but the relationship will require extra attention and may come with additional restrictions or responsibilities.

☐ While my teen is in high school, they cannot date someone who is more than two grades/years older or younger.

☐ Dating someone who is more than two grades/years older or younger may be permitted, but it requires extra conversation and consideration and may come with additional restrictions and responsibilities.

☐ Other:

22. Have I done a good job communicating these standards to my teen?

☐ Yes

☐ No, I've never sat down and reviewed my expectations with my child.

☐ My child isn't old enough to date yet.

☐ Other:

23. Have I communicated with my teen what disciplinary steps will be in our home if the standards are not honored?

☐ Yes

☐ No

☐ I don't set consequences in advance. Discipline is based on the situation.

☐ Other:

24. If I think my teen is in an unhealthy or detrimental relationship, I should: (check all that apply)

☐ Sit down and talk to my teen about what I have observed and what my concerns are, but then let them make the decision. It's their relationship.

☐ Create obstacles and distractions (new hobbies, family travel, after-school activities, etc.) to help my teen refocus their efforts elsewhere. The relationship will fade on its own.

☐ Forbid my teen from dating the person.

☐ Make a more concentrated effort to get to know their date and exert a positive influence on their relationship by being present.

☐ Do nothing. This is my teen's relationship and their opportunity to learn from their own choices. I shouldn't intrude.

☐ Sit down and talk to my teen about what I have observed and what my concerns are and use that as a foundation for setting stricter boundaries on the relationship, like earlier curfews or prohibiting "alone" activities.

☐ Other:

What surprised you about yourself as you processed through these questions and your personal answers? Are there areas you need to think about more? Are there specific points you need to communicate more clearly?

If you're married, or if you have a healthy relationship with your child's other parent, sit down and talk through this list together. Where do you agree? Where do you have different opinions? How can you address those different opinions proactively so that you present a united front to your daughter or son?

TODAY'S INTERCONNECTED CULTURE

One of the unique and sometimes challenging things about today's interconnected culture is that it allows tweens and teens to gather information and establish relationships beyond their immediate circle of home and school. It's hard for us to monitor who our teens talk to when they're poking at a cell phone keyboard. It's even harder to build a connection with our kids when we're constantly competing for their time and attention— even when they're at home, alone, on the couch, or in their bedroom. Because they are so connected, peer influence is greater than ever before, and there are opinions and ideas flowing toward our kids all the time— some of which might not reflect our values or beliefs.

On some levels, our parents had it a lot easier. Our world was smaller back then (not so long ago). Our relationships were limited by time and geography, usually to those who had something fundamentally in common with us. We lived in the same neighborhoods. We had friends at school and church and through things like our sports teams, but when we went home, the external influences basically ceased, and our families became the center of our perspective.

Now, most parents will say that it's hard to get teens to break away from their screens long enough to eat dinner. The word "friend" has come to mean a lot of different things. Your tween and teen may not have even met some of their "friends" in person, yet they are "together" every waking moment of the day (or as much as we allow them to be). And those friends, generally speaking, may expose your daughter or son to different ideas and lifestyles than we would have seen back in the limited time of landlines and passing notes in math class.

I wish there was a parent connectivity app that we could simply download to connect with our tweens and teens, but that is not the case. Instead, we need to be digitally savvy to engage in their world, and look for the opportunity to establish appropriate guidelines—not arbitrary rules to squash their fun and ruin their connections, but to offer important, up-to-date, realistic ways to handle their emerging sexual curiosity, unhealthy relationship choices, and casual sexual interactions. We have to learn how to engage in their world.

WHAT'S YOUR STYLE?

Over time, trends in the "right" way to parent have swung like seasons of fashion, capitalizing on one parental fear after another. From the early "mommy wars" about the right way to potty train to the conflicting "expert" advice about how to discipline, many parents are left constantly questioning their own instincts.

But when we look beyond the latest buzzwords and influences, most psychologists say that there are four basic approaches to parenting, based on research that goes back more than fifty years.[9]

1. **Authoritarian**: *"Because I said so."* Authoritarian parents set strict rules and demand compliance, not conversation; they are more interested in how things look on the outside than how things feel inside.

2. **Authoritative**: *"Let's talk about this."* According to The Oxford Dictionary, the word authoritative means "able to be trusted as being accurate or true; reliable." Authoritative parents establish guidelines for their children to follow but are responsive to questions and tend to be nurturing and forgiving when a child makes a mistake.

3. **Permissive**: *"Whatever you want."* These are indulgent parents who rarely discipline and often praise; they are lenient, not expecting much maturity or self-control from their child. They are more interested in being a friend than an authority.

4. **Absent**: *"Don't ask me."* Absent parents provide the basic physical needs of a child but are otherwise unavailable. Typically wrapped up in their own personal lives and problems, absent parents not only don't set rules, but they also don't communicate.

Long-term studies are clear that the **authoritative** approach—which involves consistent, reliable, strategic, relationship-based parenting—produces children who are most likely to grow into happy, successful adults. But to get there, it requires a commitment from us as parents to do the hard work with our kids, every day.

Teens crave relationships! They crave someone to authentically draw them closer and make them feel loved. They want to be with someone who chooses to spend time with them and engages in their life. They want to be respected. They want to be cheered on as they mature and develop as an individual. They want to hear that it is okay for them to establish their own likes and dislikes, goals, and plans for the future. They want to be free to make some of their own choices, yet while doing so, they're often fearful and want their parents' there, just in case.

If a teen is not finding this type of support, warmth, challenge, and encouragement at home, then the danger grows that they will seek that attention elsewhere, from someone who may not have their best interest at heart.

I've observed a lot of different parenting styles over the years. It's not fair to say that one parenting style leads to more promiscuous sexual behavior or unplanned pregnancy, because there are plenty of other factors contributing to a teen's choices. But personally—and this is only my opinion—I believe that being too authoritarian, too permissive, or altogether absent does not help your son or daughter make healthy choices.

Parents, your teen needs specific, age-appropriate guidelines, and more importantly, they need you to offer consistent, precommunicated follow-through if the guidelines are not adhered to. One of the hardest decisions to make as a parent of a teen is what boundaries to set, because once they are set, you have to be ready to and willing to enforce them—and sometimes endure them—yourself.

More than likely, there will be some hard times for you, as the parent, while your teen experiments with understanding the guidelines, the effects of their own behaviors, and their personal need for healthy boundaries. In the midst of the hard times, remember that you're the adult. You're older and wiser, and you have perspective your son or daughter doesn't have. You love your teen, so you're willing to support them as they learn to value your parenting style and why you have such guidelines in place.

HOW CAN I EXPECT MY KIDS TO WAIT IF I DIDN'T?

Opening up a conversation with your tween and teen about appropriate sexual boundaries may bring up some difficult issues about your own teen years. After all, when parents of today's tweens and teens were in high school, the rates of teen sexual activity were actually *higher* than they are now,[10] so statistically, chances are a lot of you made some embarrassing or uncomfortable decisions that you'd rather not confess to your daughter or son. What is a parent with a past full of sexual activity to do?

Hiding from the subject of sex isn't helping your teen navigate their own situations. As a parent, you have the opportunity to use whatever your past is as a springboard to possibly change your teen's future for the better. Some kids are more willing to own up to their struggles if they hear their parents admit their own shortcomings.

Before you talk to your teen, take the time for self-reflection, which provides an opportunity to identify and process through any baggage you may be carrying. I'm not saying you need to do a complete deconstruction where you are obligated to analyze *every last thing* from your own teen years. But be honest with yourself about any personal insecurities and mistakes you've made that may affect how you approach your teen's future. If you're not sure where to start, or if there are painful things that you don't know how to work through, consider seeking help from a counselor.

Every story is unique, but here are some general guidelines for approaching this delicate subject:

- If you're married, talk to your spouse in advance about what you will or won't share with your children. It's imperative that parents are in agreement about what will be shared and what will remain unsaid. Adding marital stress to this conversation doesn't help your teen make good decisions.

- Consider what from your past will add value to your teen's future. When you talk to your teen, focus on their future and on their present needs and situations. Be honest about your past if it comes up or is relevant, but remember, this conversation isn't about you.

- Stay focused on the dangers prevalent in today's culture. Educate yourself so that you are prepared to present the facts pertaining to unplanned pregnancy, sexually transmitted infections, and the emotional side effects connected to teen sexual activity.

- If you have more than one child, understand that what you share with one should eventually be shared with all of them. Don't play favorites.

- Keep your stories and descriptions general. Conversations about sex are situations where you *don't* want to hear from your teen, "TMI, Mom and Dad!"

Talking to our teens in a way that makes us feel vulnerable is not easy. For that matter, none of the things we've talked about in this chapter are easy. They touch on some of the deepest parts of how you see yourself as a parent and how you want your relationship with your daughter or son to mature in these next few years. But be brave. You can do it. Your kids desperately need you to ask the hard questions and commit to being there for them in these years of transition and change.

In the chapters that follow, I'll give you tools and suggestions for how to navigate specific facts, questions, and scenarios. But the real choices are up to you. You were chosen as the perfect parent for your child. No one else can fill your role.

PART 2: LET'S TALK ABOUT S-E-X

Help! My seventeen-year-old son, a senior, has been in a relationship with his almost-fifteen-year-old girlfriend since last spring. They are very cute together and treat each other well. They spend every moment together, at our home or at hers. The girlfriend's mom and I (we are both single parents) communicate and have agreed on rules and curfews.

Today I stumbled across a text he sent her last night for their eight-month "anniversary." The text is a long list of sweet memories…including a couple of references to sleepovers, showering together, and having sex. Wait! When did they ever have the time and space to do this?! There was also a remembrance about an embarrassing trip to the grocery store to buy condoms—the clerk was a kid they knew.

We've had the "sex talk," and my son is a good kid. But clearly he has been with her when he's told me he was sleeping over at his buddy's house. Her mom works long hours, so there are "sneaking in" opportunities. I'm upset about the lying, and I'm worried about the young age of his girlfriend. What should I do next? I'm freaking out. What if he gets her pregnant?

3

THIS IS YOUR KID'S BRAIN ON HORMONES

IN THIS chapter, we'll review "the basics," with some frank facts and a few statistics to help you prepare to be the parent your tween and teen need. For some, this may be a review; for others, this may be new information. Regardless, I suggest reading this chapter to make sure you're up to speed.

Going through puberty is different than being a parent watching your child go through puberty. Many of us have chosen to forget our own awkward pubescent experience, and yet the changes and rapid development of our sons' and daughters' bodies produces uncomfortable reminders. For many of us, it seems like only yesterday we were diapering and dressing them. So how are we already facing changing bodies and mood swings? This is commonly a time of confusion, fear, sadness, and anticipation for both the tween and parent, somehow all wrapped together in one hormone-fueled package.

To start, let's define puberty, adolescence, and sexuality. For tweens and teens, they're used to their bodies changing. Not only have they lost a set of teeth, but for their whole lives, they've had to get new shoes and clothes every six months because they're growing. This means pubescent and adolescent changes are uncomfortable and awkward, but not necessarily foreign. But sexuality is different; it goes beyond the obvious physical changes to include emotions and desires. For many individuals, sexuality also includes a spiritual side. We know this, but do our daughters and sons?

- **Puberty** is the stage of life at which a child turns into a young man or young woman, when the reproductive organs become functional and secondary sex characteristics (i.e. enlarged breast in females, and facial hair and adam's apple in males) develop.

- **Adolescence** is the period between puberty and adulthood, the last stage of physical body growth.

- **Sexuality** is a complex aspect of our personality and "self" defined by our sexual thoughts, desires, and intimate longings for another person.

HOW THE BODY CHANGES

Boys and girls experience different rates of change, with boys usually lagging about two years behind girls. Because of this, parents should be on the lookout for natural development signs and begin explaining the facts about the body, sexuality, and the changes that are going to happen **prior** to these developmental changes taking place. This will ease the confusion once it begins.

Changes include:

For girls: body hair appears, breasts develop, hips broaden, waist narrows, and the reproductive organs develop further (uterus and vagina grow larger). Teen girls may experience weight gain, mood swings, crying spells, and feelings of agitation that are related to the fluctuation of hormones within their bodies. Menstruating can bring a number of side effects including headaches, backaches, cramps, nausea, and water retention.

For boys: body hair appears, shoulders broaden, muscle mass and bone length increase, hips narrow, voice deepens, and the reproductive organs develop further (penis and testes get larger and the scrotum darkens in color). Boys experience spontaneous erections frequently because of high or fluctuating testosterone levels. They also experience nocturnal emissions (wet dreams) with involuntary orgasms and ejaculations during sleep. An erection can be caused by having to urinate, being excited, experiencing sexual arousal, or friction from clothing. It's also common for one testicle to position lower than the other, to ensure sperm are maintained at the proper temperature.

For both girls and boys:

- Skin becomes oilier and thickens so that pores become plugged, which leads to pimples and potential acne issues.

- New sweat glands produce perspiration when the teen is nervous, afraid, or participating in physical activity. This can lead to increased body odor.

- Bodies grow to full height and strength increases.

- Nipples may darken in color.

- Body produces sexual hormones.

- Sexual and romantic feelings are strong and frequent; dreams occur often about friends and sex.

KEY TOPICS TO DISCUSS WITH YOUR TWEENS

As teens move through adolescence and into the dating and relationship years, they'll be ready for you to tackle the Pure Sexual Freedom model, and all of the topics found on the following pages. But before that, you can lay a strong foundation of trust and information, starting right at the beginning of puberty.

To assist, here are some key topics that preteens need to understand as they enter into puberty.

Note: I use a broad age range here for puberty, because there's no one universal age when every child is ready for these topics. As I mentioned earlier, the average age a child hits puberty is getting younger. But some kids are also "late bloomers" and are nowhere ready to talk about these things at eight, or even at ten. When you think about when and how to talk to your own child, make your decisions based on who they are, how they are specifically developing, and whether or not the tweens and teens around them are developing, rather than an arbitrary date on the calendar.

Ages 8-12: What a Boy Should Know

- Body changes (height, weight, voice deepening)

- Skin changes (breakouts, clogged pores)

- Growth of body hair (shaving)

- Hygiene needs due to hormonal changes (deodorant)

- Nocturnal emissions (wet dreams)

- How to handle emotional changes based on hormones

- Understanding basic male and female reproductive organs and how a female gets pregnant

- The difference between inner beauty and outer beauty

- Unhealthy or inaccurate depictions of alcohol, sex, and drugs in the media

Ages 8-12: What a Girl Should Know

- Menstruation

- Breast development (wearing bras)

- Skin changes (breakouts, clogged pores)

- Growth of body hair (shaving)

- Hygiene needs due to hormonal changes (deodorant)

- How to handle emotional changes based on hormones

- Understanding basic male and female reproductive organs and how a female gets pregnant

- The difference between inner beauty and outer beauty

- Unhealthy or inaccurate depictions of alcohol, sex, and drugs in the media

Tweens, boys and girls alike, are naturally overwhelmed with what's happening to their bodies. It's important that both parents, if possible, are available and supportive during this time and that you remain calm and guide them through the natural process of development.

Books are great ways to start the conversation, and to provide basic medical information, but remember that your son or daughter needs a relationship with you too. Be proactive. Consider reading a book with them, and talk with them about what they're reading, what they're feeling, and what you're observing.

HOW THE BRAIN CHANGES

Puberty changes more than just a child's outward appearance. It also directly affects their brain and hormones—and thus, their thoughts and feelings. During this emotional stage of life, it's common for teens to genuinely believe the world revolves around them. At the same time, their emotions are driving them with a desperate need for acceptance and a sense of belonging. They're often living an imaginary melodrama on a daily basis.

We're born with a hundred billion neurons in our brain, with each having an average of ten thousand branches. The possible number of connections is about one quadrillion—that's a 1 followed by *15 zeros*. While a baby is developing inside the womb, 17% of the brain is being "hardwired." That is why certain behaviors are universal. For instance, in every country and culture, babies normally have the ability to make noise—but what language they learn depends on their particular experiences. The other 83% of the brain is "soft-wired." This means that paths and patterns are formed in response to experiences. When experiences cause specific neurons to connect branches into pathways, it starts building patterns for how that particular brain uniquely functions.[11]

During puberty, teen hormonal changes wreak havoc on the brain as neural pathways increase.[12] This very natural process opens the door for new learning, which is good, but the increase can also lead to a lack of critical thinking, which can be dangerous.

The dramatic brain changes undergone during this stage of development—formed by both genetics and experience—mean that a teen's brain will not be fully developed until he or she is about twenty-three to twenty-five years old.[13] Research actually shows that the parts of the brain that use critical thinking—which is disciplined, clear, rational, open-minded, and informed by evidence[14]—are still developing through the teen years and are the least-used areas of the teen brain.[15] With these parts of the brain still under development, teens do not automatically know how to process decisions step-by-step or consider long-term benefits or consequences in order to make reasoned decisions.

Emotions are usually displayed through actions rather than words. It is common during this transitional time for teens to wonder things like: *What does sex really feel like? Will a boyfriend/girlfriend make me happy? If I have a boyfriend/girlfriend, will I be more popular?* Pondering such questions about the opposite sex leads to an intense *feeling* deemed worthy of action.

The extraordinary changes happening internally can also cause a hormonal teen to behave in an explosive manner and make impulsive decisions. Feelings become more intense, little things get amplified, and fears are more frightening. Also, pleasure is more exciting, irritations are more distressing, and frustrations are more intolerable. Every experience seems to be super-sized!

DEALING WITH MELTDOWNS

Hormonal surges and fluctuating feelings during puberty and adolescence often lead to emotional meltdowns, in which an emotional teen responds to a small frustration in a way that's way out of context. There may be tears or shouting or impulsive, hurtful words. It may feel like you've moved back to those tantrums from the "terrible twos." As the parent, it can be hard to remember that this is a normal part of this stage of life and is driven by physiological changes that your teen can't fully control.

However, it's also our responsibility as parents to set limits and to teach our teens how to respond in a healthy and productive manner. If you find yourself in the midst of a tween/teen meltdown—related to puberty, sex, dating, or other issues—consider the following:

1. Recognize the meltdown as early as possible. Once you realize you are in the midst of one, stop talking and take a deep breath. Acknowledge to yourself that you are dealing with a natural, typical tween/teen meltdown.

2. Determine if this is an **old** issue that has risen again, or if this is a **new** issue.

   - If it's an **old** issue, calmly state that this has already been discussed, and let your tween know that you will not revisit your decision. Tell them that they can talk as much as they want about the situation, but they need to do so somewhere else, either in their room or otherwise alone.

   - If this is a **new** issue, try not to be an audience. Stay calm and cool, and ask them to explain their concerns with words. Listen without reacting, take a break, and think about it if you need to.

   - If you are married, make sure you and your spouse prepare and present a united front and are ready to support one another. Then, state the plan of action and move on without lecturing or arguing.

3. If your tween or teen has broken household expectations during the meltdown, take a break before you determine appropriate discipline. Match the correction to the infraction.

4. Remember that the goal is to develop their character, not to win or to damage their spirit.

As you consistently use a calm, predetermined approach, it's likely that your tween will mature and learn how to work through these types of meltdowns on their own, until they are happening less and less.

THE TEEN BRAIN IN A DIGITAL ERA

Science has uncovered additional aspects about the teen brain that many of us might never have considered, but which affect our teens every day. We're only starting now to understand how widespread access to electronic technology is reshaping the ways younger generations think.[16]

The digital culture is quickly diminishing natural forms of interaction within the home. Remember when the family would gather around the dinner table and talk about their days? Well, maybe it was more like the family gathered around the TV and talked about what was on that night, but it was still a shared experience. For many families now, having dinner together means everyone's sitting in a room, staring at their own personal screens. They're all communicating—but not with the people in the room.

This digital prioritization has begun to change the way young people relate to each other and to the world around them. Studies show that younger generations are far less linear—responding completely to one stimuli before moving on to another—because of the interconnected, multitasking nature of digital learning and social networking. They multitask, juggle multiple conversations at once, and never give anything— or anyone—their full attention. Through social media, teens can fluidly shift conversations from Facebook to Twitter to Instagram to text on their phones. They see the world through a nonlinear "virtual space" as much as in IRL—"in real life"—and they do so fluidly, while maybe doing a little bit of homework on the side.

Digital, nonlinear relationships have spilled over into the dating world. Too many teens believe they can beta test their relationships by relying on rigorously crafted social media and online dating profiles and can undo a mistake with a click of the "edit" or "delete" button.

The loss of in-person interaction can harm a teen's ability to perceive/ predict real world consequences. If you can "unfriend" a person or Photoshop an embarrassing picture, then they think every decision can be altered after the fact. Cyberbullying, for instance, has become a teenage epidemic because teens, feeling anonymous and invisible on the other end of a screen, say horrible things without observing the hurt that their actions cause in real life. Those teens who are ignorant of the emotional consequences of conversational interactions will be ill prepared to handle the larger consequences of risky life choices.

ADVICE FOR PARENTING IN THIS DIGITAL WORLD

The stakes here are high. The digital world could easily eclipse our teen's evolving maturity and possibly impair or stunt their judgment at a critical stage of life. But whether we like it or not, the digital era is not going away, and a teen's ultimate success related to the digital world is dependent on harnessing its power in a positive way. Here's what you can do to help:

- **Set the standard for the technology in your home early.** Teaching your child how to behave responsibly with the avalanche of information available to them is an absolute must.

- **Monitor your teen's phone, tablet, and computer to see what apps they're installing and what websites they're visiting.** Take the time to understand what programs and services your teen is using, and gauge their age appropriateness. Every week it seems like the media is touting a new, dangerous or unhealthy program that encourages users to engage in sexually suggestive behavior, often with strangers.

- **Choose and install monitoring software with parental controls on your teen's computer and phone so that you can block inappropriate sites.** Here are a few that get good reviews: Parental Controls for iPad and iPhone, uKnowKids social and mobile monitoring app, Spy Agent, Web Watcher, PC Pandora.

- **Help your teen learn to stop and think before they reveal personal information.** Teach them about phishing scams (when someone attempts to acquire private information like usernames and passwords by masquerading as a trustworthy entity) and predators, but also help them understand that they are worth a certain level of privacy. They don't need to share every thought, fact, or embarrassing action, even with the friends they trust. Self-reflection before self-revelation is an important tool for teens to learn.

- **Don't judge your teen's online connectivity**. As long as your teen isn't indulging in unhealthy behavior, keep an open mind about the new games, programs, and communication channels they choose. Understand that their world is digital. Ask questions. Consider creating your own social media accounts to engage with your teen on their turf. Let them know you want to partner with them. Have them help you with the digital ways of our current world. They will feel intelligent, and you will feel aware.

- **Teach your child to be kind**. We expect our kids to play fair and treat others with respect in the real world. Set the same expectations for the digital world. Do not tolerate any bullying or abusive behavior.

- **Prompt your child to maintain balance**. Help your teen learn how to balance their time in reference to the digital world. Turn off all the screens by a certain time each night or a full day every weekend. Live by example!

- **Prioritize real relationships**. Regularly remind your teen that the real world happens beyond their screens and that the people they're talking to are real humans. Encourage activities and outings that build real, face-to-face relationships with your teen's peers, and help them see they can't test friendships and make changes like they do with their usernames.

We know that developing a genuine parent-teen relationship is important, but in the roller coaster of changes, it won't happen haphazardly. It's difficult and requires time, intention, patience, and creativity. But it can be done!

4

WHEN WE TALK ABOUT SEX...

I N THIS mixed-up, highly emotional, confusing time of a tween or teen's life, what pushes them to sex? I've asked hundreds of them. Here are some of the answers I've heard over and over:

If I do it, my friends will think I'm cool.

If he paid for the date, I'm supposed to have sex.

I get the high five from my buddies in the locker room if I 'get some.'

It just happens.

The kids at my school who have sex are popular.

If someone will have sex with me, then I'll know that I'm good looking.

My family is so messed up, it doesn't matter what I do.

I love him, and he loves me.

I tried to say no before and he didn't stop, so why bother.

I'm old enough.

If I get pregnant, he won't break up with me.

I'm so lonely, and it makes me feel good.

Sex looks so awesome in all of the movies and TV shows that I watch.

I'm mad at my parents.

One thing that never ceases to amaze me is that most of the young people I talk to genuinely believe that sex is just a physical act and that engaging in it is no big deal, or that it's a rite of passage, like getting a driver's license or taking the SATs.

Of course they do! Who in our current culture is telling them otherwise? The news is full of explicit descriptions of the sexual exploits of everyone from politicians to pastors, movie stars to college football players. Movies and TV no longer shy away from teens having well-lit, awkward-but-charming sexual encounters, often with emotional soundtracks in the background.

It certainly seems like sex is a harmless physical act and that "everyone's doing it."

What society doesn't show our kids is what happens next. The celebrities apologize—or don't—and stay famous. The fictional stories all have happy endings, with either a happy couple or, at worst, the love and support of friends and family after a breakup. Our teens don't see the impact of STIs or the long-term challenges of teen pregnancy or the upheaval of post-abortion symptoms. And they definitely don't see the long-term emotional effects: the depression, the shame, the sense of loss that comes from rushed intimacy.

Yes, every human being was made for relationships. According to the Maslow hierarchy of needs, a theory in psychology that focuses on human motivation, humans need to feel a sense of acceptance and belonging among their peers or social groups and they need to love and be loved—both sexually and non-sexually—by others.[17] But here's the catch: the physical act of sex does not fulfill that need.

Society's hyper-sexualization leads our daughters and sons to believe that those needs for acceptance and love can be met regardless of who they're "doing it" with, or whether or not it's respectful and healthy, as long as everyone consents. The emotional, psychological, mental, and for many, spiritual components of sexuality are rarely addressed. Most teens don't fully understand that sexual interaction is not just a merging of bodies; it's also a merging of souls.

What are you doing to counter the false messages and enticing images being thrown at your daughter or son? Are you prepared to talk about the things they're hearing and seeing?

In such a graphic world, the "birds and bees" talk is no longer going to cut it. If you're going to communicate, you need to know what they're talking about and what they're hearing from the world around them. For many parents, that starts with expanding your vocabulary.

If we're going to be part of the conversation, we need to be able to talk about sexual activity and sexual intercourse from an honest, frank, and medically accurate perspective.

WHAT IS AT-RISK SEXUAL ACTIVITY?

Years ago, when I started teaching sexual health, I spent most of my time talking to students about what they *couldn't* or *shouldn't* do. Today, many of the ninth graders in my classes know more about sex than I knew when I got married. They're savvy about experimenting with boundaries. Today's tweens and teens are comfortable talking about these topics and are more interested in talking about what they *can* do—how far can they push things and still be safe?

Here's what I tell them—and what you should know. **Medically and legally speaking, any act of sexual penetration is considered sexual intercourse**. That includes:

- **Vaginal penetration**—When the penis penetrates the vagina.

- **Oral sex**—Stimulation of the genitals using the mouth.

- **Anal sex**—Penetration of the anus, usually by the penis.

This can be a controversial topic. Plenty of teens (and adults) will try to justify their behaviors by limiting their definition of sex to only intercourse of a penis and vagina—or even try to say that sex is only ejaculation into a vagina. To protect their reputation or to assuage their morals, they rely on "technical virginity"—or what we used to call "doing everything but." That leaves a lot of room for incredibly risky behavior that does not fall into this limited definition of sex.

Instead of asking "Are you having sex?" a better question is "Are you engaged in at-risk sexual activity?"

From a public health perspective, the **physical risks** from sexual activity start well before intercourse, when a person **touches any part of**

another person's body that is normally covered by underwear, which includes skin-to-skin contact, and/or **any time body fluids come into contact with body openings.**

This is often referred to as the "no zone" or the "underwear zone." Everything that happens here has risks.

IS "SAFE" SEX SAFE?

Throughout this book, we will discuss how teens benefit most from intentional *prevention education*, leading them to not engage in sexual activity. When I have conversations with teens about sex, the word prevention often leads them to believe I am referring to "safe" sex. I'm not! I'm referring to **preventing sexual activity and sexual intercourse**, not simply preventing the potential *physical consequences* of engaging in sexual activity and sexual intercourse.

The tweens and teens I talk to justify their experimentation with all sorts of logic, which usually comes down to "but we're being safe." They've been taught—by their peers, by the media, and sometimes by well-intentioned parents and doctors—that condoms or other forms of birth control are the solution. But a condom protects a couple from pregnancy only about 84% of the time, and other forms of birth control, like pills and IUDs, don't protect against STIs.[18]

Yes, it's safer, but not necessarily *safe*.

Beyond the significant, life-altering physical consequences, teen sexual activity can have devastating psychological, social, and financial consequences, which we'll explore more in the next chapter. A condom can't protect the heart. A thin layer of latex is no match for potential feelings of fear, guilt, embarrassment, shame, or confusion—even if it's used consistently and correctly every time, which is highly unlikely among the teen population.

There's no such thing as "safe" sex for adolescents whose bodies and brains are still developing. Sex is an activity that teens simply don't have the maturity to handle, to fully understand what they're doing, or to deal with the consequences they may face.

It's important to address this here because parents often send confusing mixed messages about "safe" sex to their teens. They encourage their teens to not have sex and to pursue what we call Pure Sexual Freedom, but then tell them that if they're going to have sex anyway, at least use a condom. This is similar to telling your teen to be home by curfew—but then asking them to at least call if they're going to stay out all night. It's like grounding your son or daughter from driving the car and then telling her the keys are in the kitchen drawer if she decides to go somewhere.

Teens have a tendency to use selective listening, and that will include what you say about sex. So parents, before you even start a conversation with your teen, make sure you know what you believe. Is a condom or birth control pill really what you want them to take away from your conversation? What outcome are you looking for: to have a teen who chooses **not** to have sex or to have a teen who chooses to engage in "safer" sex?

I understand that just reading this information can be uncomfortable and talking to your son or daughter may seem overwhelming. My hope is that it provides you with perspective and encourages you to do a status check within your own home. Our parental influence matters—unequivocally! Teens may shuffle their feet, grimace, roll their eyes, and look bored when you broach these topics—but I assure you, they're listening.

The shifting culture doesn't change the fact that you can **leverage** your influence and **empower** your teen to make healthy choices. Peer groups will impact some of the choices your teen makes, but positive, ongoing, intentional involvement in your teen's life, which is the primary factor that guides them and influences their direction, will play a much greater role.

5

SEX AND CONSEQUENCES

TWEENS and teens, with their still-developing minds, imagine all kinds of benefits to diving into sexual activity. They think it will bring them love, acceptance, and the respect of their peers. The reality couldn't be further from that.

Sexual activity comes with a host of consequences, which can drastically change a teen's present and future. As parents, it's our responsibility to educate our teens to better understand that they can choose their choices, but they can't choose their consequences.

But first, we need to better understand for ourselves what those consequences are—including physical, psychological, social, and financial.

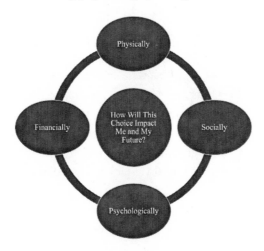

PHYSICAL CONSEQUENCES

PREGNANCY

The first thing that both parents and teens think about when I mention
the consequences of teen sex is unplanned pregnancy. Recent data shows
that American teen girls between fifteen and nineteen years old experience approximately 614,000 pregnancies annually.[19] An alarming statis-
tic, no doubt, and even more worrisome when coupled with the fact that
pregnant teenagers may have a higher risk of the following:

- Minimal or inadequate prenatal care (especially pregnant teens
  without supportive families)

- Pregnancy-induced hypertension (high blood pressure)

- Preeclampsia

- Premature birth

- Low birth weight babies

- Postpartum depression

And for teens who continue to engage in at-risk sexual activity during the pregnancy, their babies have a higher risk of sexually transmitted
infections such as chlamydia and HIV.[20]

STD/STIS

Pregnancy is just the tip of the iceberg when it comes to the physical
consequences of sexual activity. Sexually active teens today risk more
than thirty different kinds of bacteria, viruses, and parasites that cause
sexually transmitted infections (STIs).[21] A person can have an STI without having obvious symptoms of disease, which makes this a broader,
and more dangerous, category than sexually transmitted diseases (STDs).
STDs result from damage caused by an STI that has progressed. Although all STDs are preceded by STIs, not all STIs result in the development of STDs.

According to the Centers for Disease Control and Prevention, nearly
half of the twenty million sexually transmitted infections that occur each

year in the United States are among young people ages fifteen to twenty-four.[22] Approximately 3.2 million teenage girls, one in four, between the ages of fourteen and nineteen is infected with at least one of the common sexually transmitted infections: human papillomavirus (HPV), chlamydia, herpes simplex virus, and trichomoniasis.[23]

Most STIs are transmitted through the exchange of sexual fluids through vaginal, anal, or oral sex, but some can be passed on through skin-to-skin genital contact. STIs can cause a wide range of health problems, from mild irritations to serious illness. STIs such as chlamydia and gonorrhea are major causes of infertility, pelvic inflammatory disease, and adverse pregnancy outcomes.[24] Between 50%-70% of people with a STI do not know they have the infection because they have no symptoms.[25] And some sexually transmitted infections are incurable and can lead to life-long complications or even death.[26]

THE INTERVENTION OF VACCINES

Discussing the epidemic of STIs and STDs with parents always leads to questions related to the vaccines. Protection against hepatitis B and HPV is currently available. Reports say that vaccines for herpes and HIV are advancing, though no viable vaccine candidates for either infection have yet emerged. Research into vaccines for chlamydia, gonorrhea, syphilis, and trichomoniasis is in earlier stages.

Vaccines do represent major advances in the prevention of STIs. Hepatitis B is a virus that can cause chronic liver disease and cancer. The vaccine against hepatitis B, which can be transmitted through sexual contact, is now included in the infant immunization process.

The three-dose HPV vaccine, typically under the brand name Gardasil or Cervarix, protects from the rapidly spreading human papillomavirus and some of its more dangerous effects, especially cervical cancer. Although signs of infection are not always seen, studies show that up to 65% of Americans have been exposed to the HPV virus. Men and women are both carriers of the disease, while women bear a majority of the long-term risks.[27]

Most family doctors and pediatricians follow the standard of care recommendations of the American Academy of Pediatrics (AAP) and the Centers for Disease Control and Prevention (CDC), which recommends that all girls and boys between eleven and twelve are vaccinated against HPV. The CDC also reports this vaccination is effective when given to women up to age twenty-six, and to men up to twenty-one.[28] The purpose of the HPV vaccine is not to encourage or condone sexual activity; it's to reduce the dangerous effects related to it. The prompting by most doctors for this vaccination provides a wonderful opportunity for parents to ask the doctor questions, educate themselves and have conversations with their tweens and teens concerning the overall risks connected to engaging in sexual activity.

Another important point to consider related to the HPV vaccination is that sexually transmitted infections aren't only passed during unhealthy sexual encounters. A vaccine could protect your daughter or son not only from the consequences of their own behavior but also from any secondhand consequences that their future spouse might bring into their marriage. We don't know what journey our future son- or daughter-in-law is on, and it is possible they could bring the weight of past decisions and unhealthy choices into a marriage.

PSYCHOLOGICAL CONSEQUENCES

The psychological consequences of teen sexual activity are often overlooked because it's hard to measure a person's thoughts and feelings or to evaluate the causes of what we feel. The teen years are already full of emotional highs and lows, so when a young person chooses to be sexually active, it adds confusion and stress to an already perplexing stage of life. Sexual activity opens up areas of vulnerability that a teen isn't developmentally ready to handle and exposes their most intimate part to another person who also probably isn't mature enough to handle it. Teens are more likely to impulsively give all they can to a physical relationship, totally exposing themselves, and only start to grapple with the implications later.

Many of the young people that I interact with—both girls and boys—who admit to being sexually active express worry, guilt, fear of the future, and loss of self-respect. They're distracted, disconnecting from their friends, at odds with their families, and their grades are often falling. Research shows that sexually active girls are nearly three times more likely to feel depressed and have attempted suicide[29] and sexually active boys are two times more likely to be depressed and nearly *eight times* more likely to have attempted suicide than their peers who are not sexually active.[30]

Most teen relationships crumble under the fear and the breakdown of trust. This often leads to questions like "What type of feelings, memories, and regrets will result because of the choices I've made?"

Symptomatically, sexually active teens often lose hope, thinking it is not possible to start over or find a positive path for their future. This false misconception usually leads to additional unhealthy behavior and additional consequences.

SOCIAL CONSEQUENCES

When it comes to the social implications of sexual activity, our teens live under the shadow of a painful double standard. Teen boys regularly report that they were encouraged to experiment sexually, not only by the media but also their peers, older brothers and friends, and sometimes even their fathers. Sex and the ability to "get some," they're implicitly and explicitly told, is a sign of their manhood.

Even when boys intuitively know that they're not ready for this kind of intimacy, they're led to believe that how far they go physically—and how much they're willing to talk about—will determine where they rank in terms of respect and approval amongst their male peers. The pressure is high for them to experiment (and exaggerate). Boys who don't "kiss and tell" don't get those high fives in the locker room.

Sadly, we still live in a culture where boys build their reputations based on the stories of their exploits, while girls lose theirs.

I'll never forget the story I heard of a tenth-grade boy who went out with the guys one weekend. They met up with some girls, and one thing led to another, and the boy "scored." When that young man jumped into the car to head home, his friends whistled, cheered, and gave him high fives.

The girl, on the other hand, was in eighth grade, somebody's little sister flaunting "her stuff" to cover up her insecurity around the older kids. She and her friends had been excited about meeting up with the guys all week. Then, in the midst of the flirting, and the compliments, and the music playing in the background, she went a lot further than she'd ever gone…or intended to go. It all happened pretty quickly. When she met back up with her friends to go home, the questions started flying. Only no one was cheering for her. Her "friends" weren't even making eye contact. Then her phone started to buzz. The gossip had begun. Photos had been taken and sent, and before she could even process through what she did, she'd been labeled as a "slut."

It's not okay that we have this double standard, but it's the world your teens live in.

Too many teen girls make the mistake of thinking sexual activity will provide love and security. A teen girl may throw herself into a "hot and heavy" relationship, alienating all of her friends in the process. Or she may make an impulsive mistake in a moment of vulnerability, "hooking up" with someone to get their short-term approval and attention. Either way, most of the time, she will find herself the center of rumors, isolation, and even bullying. Either way, she ends up alone.

I hear stories over and over of a girl who was sure that if she went "just a little further," the boy would stay with her. Or she sees the perceived happy endings that the girls on TV seem to experience or all the attention that the popular girls get from boys, and she just wants to know how it feels. Instead, the opposite is usually the case. Most sexually active teen girls struggle with not only the personal consequences of their behavior but also with the negative impacts on their friendships. Friends scatter, either in disapproval or to protect their own reputations from the vicious high school gossip mill.

For the sexually active teen girl, this peer rejection often drives her to lower self-respect, increased vulnerability, and more poor choices. If the only people who like her anymore are the boys who are interested in her body, then that's where she'll go to get the attention she craves.

FINANCIAL CONSEQUENCES

Having a baby is expensive—you probably remember that from your own experience, but teens often have no concept of what they'll pay if they bring a new life into the world. Hospital deliveries in the United States cost approximately $3,500 per stay, according to the Agency for Healthcare Research and Quality Healthcare Cost and Utilization Project. Add in prenatal, delivery-related and postpartum healthcare, and the cost of childbirth is over $8,000.[31] The average cost of raising a child born in 2013 until they are eighteen is approximately **$245,340** (or $304,480, adjusted for projected inflation), according to the U.S. Department of Agriculture. That includes housing, food, transportation, clothing, health care, education, child care, and miscellaneous expenses like haircuts and cell phones, but not big-ticket items like college.[32]

Not only are there initial medical costs for what may be a high-risk pregnancy, but there are also lifelong implications for both the teen parents and their child:

- Only 40% of teen moms who choose to parent their child finish high school.[33] According to the American Congress of Obstetricians and Gynecologists, teen fathers are also less likely to finish high school than their childless peers.[34]

- Over time, teen fathers earn 10%-15% less annually than male teens who wait to have children, according to the National Campaign to Prevent Teen Pregnancy.[35]

- A child born to an unmarried teen mother who has not finished high school is nine times more likely to be poor than a child born to an adult parent who is married and has graduated from high school.[36]

- The child of teen parents is also more likely to drop out of high school.[37]

- 80% of the teen girls who drop out of school based on pregnancy will receive government assistance.[38] According to a recent report, teen pregnancy and childbearing in the United States costs tax payers nearly $11 billion per year.[39]

Pregnancy is not the only sexual consequence with a financial impact. Teens who contract a sexually transmitted infection or disease face medical bills, which can be daunting for conditions that require long-term treatment. The Centers for Disease Control and Prevention estimate that the treatment of STIs in the United States costs $15.6 billion each year.[40]

While an unplanned pregnancy or an STI presents an immediate financial concern, there are added financial repercussions to sexual activity that are harder to quantify—but no less real than those listed above. Research shows that teens who engage in sexual activity are more likely to either drop out or be expelled from school than teens that do not have sex. Additionally, teens who do not have sex are nearly twice as likely to graduate from college.[41] Since high school and college degrees are directly tied to a person's lifetime earning potential, a teen's sexual activity can have far-reaching effects on his or her financial future.

These are staggering implications for a sexually active teen, but without their parents' help, most teens are not mature enough or educated enough to fully understand the magnitude of the problem.

"DO YOU WANT TO HAVE A GREAT SEX LIFE?"

All of this information sounds dire. But the point is not to scare you, or your teen. Trust me—throwing a bunch of statistics at them about a potential danger doesn't get you very far. Teens are experts at believing "that can't happen to me."

So when I'm talking to teens, I take a different approach. I ask them: **"Do you want to increase your chance of experiencing great sex?"**

Once they pick up their jaws from the floor, we begin a conversation that greatly increases a teen's chance of waiting and not engaging in sexual activity, until the time when they're old enough for true intimacy and a lifetime commitment. That, I assure them, is where the great sex happens.

When teens choose to engage in at-risk sexual activity (often termed casual sex), they potentially damage their capacity to experience the true intimacy that they are worthy of. They're endangering and possibly even risking their ability to engage in what they should get to experience someday, which is great sex. In short, **they could be ruining their own sex life!**

Parents, your teen needs you to have these types of conversations with them. Don't hesitate to break it down and walk them through *all* of the potential consequences of sexual activity. There's a lot more risk than they may have thought about.

PART 3: PURE SEXUAL FREEDOM

Leslie's story:

At fourteen, I started to feel a lot of confusion, loneliness, and a huge void in my life. I was faced with a lot of temptations, and I started to hang out with boys, go out more, and eventually I started having sex. All my friends were doing it! I wanted to know and experience what they were feeling and doing. After, I was surprised; it didn't feel like I thought it was going to.

I felt used, which led me to doing drugs and drinking alcohol, yet those things didn't seem to make me feel better. In fact, they made me feel worse. This was my life for five years, and my parents didn't have a clue.

It was amazing that I hadn't gotten pregnant, and one day I thought for sure the test would be positive. I sat in the counseling room at the pregnancy clinic by myself. No one knew I was there, not even my boyfriend. If I was pregnant, I wanted to figure it out on my own.

The nurse came into my room and shared that the pregnancy test was negative. After she left, the counselor started asking questions that no one had ever asked me before. She was kind but straightforward about the fact that I was very fortunate to not be pregnant. She asked what my plan would be if I did get pregnant. She asked me if this boy I was dating was someone I could trust to care for me. She asked if I realized that just because I had chosen to be sexually active in the past didn't mean I had to continue to be sexually active. She stated it in a way I had never really thought about. I had a choice! I could still control what my future looked like.

She gave me a step-by-step process for starting over. From that point on, I didn't have sex. It wasn't easy, and the only reason it worked was because I met with the lady at the clinic each week and she held me accountable. She told me about how valuable I am and what an incredible future I had ahead of me.

Don't get me wrong. I was still tempted, and I hung out with the wrong crowd a few times and put myself in a few vulnerable environments. But I learned the need to change my routine and to eliminate the tempting environments. I also broke up with my boyfriend. I thought this was going to be so hard, but it was easier than I anticipated. When I told him I thought I was pregnant, he questioned if it was his baby. That devastated me. Then when I told him I didn't want to have sex anymore, he got mad and said I was stupid. He even said the lady at the clinic was some religious freak who had obviously gotten a hold of me. His response confirmed that I needed to move on.

The thought of sexuality as a gift—something I can control—was a concept I couldn't fathom until I heard the message over and over. A year later I started college, and I was still surrounded by the sex scene. But I started to notice how much heartache was linked to my friends who were having sex. I had a friend get pregnant and choose to abort; I had a friend who got drunk and wasn't sure who she had sex with. The stories consistently led me to be thankful that I made a decision to change.

It hasn't been easy, but the conviction of my heart to not be sexually active until my wedding night is real. I want to be with someone who respects, loves, supports, listens, wants the best for me. I want someone who pursues me in a healthy way and who loves me for who I am, not for what I do or don't do.

6

THE PURE SEXUAL FREEDOM MODEL

TAKE heart, parents: contrary to what the media may try to make you believe, it's not inevitable that your teen will engage in dangerous sexual activity. Teens *do* have a choice, and with your help, your son or daughter *can* intentionally do what's best for their future.

Refraining from sexual activity runs against much of what our teens hear at their school and see in the media, but it's still indisputably the healthiest choice. And the message is getting through: every year, the number of teens engaging in sex decreases as intentional, evidence-based education efforts increase.[42]

Our kids are listening, but they need to hear the same message at home, as well as at school. They need us to be consistent with what we believe and with what we tell them. We tell our teens for the sake of their health they can (and should) say no to smoking, to drugs, and to drinking, but we often change our approach when it comes to sexual activity and assume that they're not capable of "just saying no."

We've come a long way since the days when you took sex ed…if your school even offered any education at all. Through the 1980s, sex education in American public schools was either nonexistent or was considered "**nondirective.**" It was based on four principles:[43]

1. Teenage sexual activity is inevitable.

2. Educators should be value-neutral regarding sex.

3. Schools should openly discuss sexual matters.

4. Sex education should teach students about contraception.

This "unbiased" approach had serious consequences; it placed students in an adult decision-making mode that they were not developmentally prepared for. It caused stress and confusion among the teen population. And, given all of the open options related to sex, it resulted in a dramatic increase in teen pregnancies and sexually transmitted infections.

Concerned by what was happening, and in the shadow of the HIV epidemic, in the 1990s schools across the country started to shift to a **directive** approach to sex education. The directive teaching style doesn't try to scare teens into making healthy choices, but rather it educates them with medically accurate evidence about the long-term effects of teen sexual activity. When the directive approach is used correctly, teens understand concepts like setting boundaries, how to say no, goal setting, the characteristics of a healthy relationship compared to the characteristics of an unhealthy relationship, the benefits of *choosing* not to be sexually active, the reality of the risks and consequences linked to teen sexual activity, and more.

My approach to teaching directive sex education is called the Pure Sexual Freedom model, which is based on the idea that every individual who chooses to date, including your teen son or daughter, deserves to experience healthy, positive dating. Pure Sexual Freedom defines what a healthy relationship is, what it looks like, and what characteristics it includes. We show teens that a healthy dating relationship is only possible if the two individuals are like-minded, respect themselves and each other, and choose to do what is truly best for one another as a whole person: **physically, psychologically, financially, and socially**.

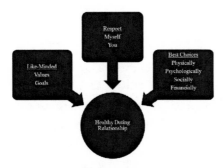

Those four categories—which we also saw in the last chapter when we explored the consequences of sexual activity—form the foundation for the Pure Sexual Freedom model, because they reflect how your daughter or son is developing and maturing during these tween and teen years.

The *physical* aspect pertains to the physical body. This is often the most familiar dimension of teen sexual activity.

The *psychological* aspect refers to the thought processes, feelings, and perceptions a person has about themselves, others, and life in general.

The *social* aspect addresses a teen's relationships with other individuals, parents and siblings, peer groups, and other social groups.

The *financial* aspect looks at what's involved, practically speaking, to live as a mature, responsible, contributing member of society.

Let's look at each of these areas in more detail, and what your role, as parents, can be.

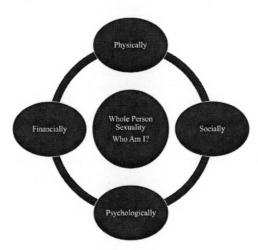

PHYSICAL

All humans are born with a powerful and innate need for physical touch. According to Dr. Matthew Hertenstein, DePauw University associate professor of psychology, scientists are finding that "Touch causes one's stress hormones, such as cortisol, to decrease while causing other hormones, such as oxytocin, to increase – thus promoting social bonding and wellness. Moreover, brain regions that are activated in anticipation of stressful events are reduced when touched by another person. Recent studies also indicate that touch can communicate such distinct emotions as love, gratitude and sympathy – just by a brief touch to the arm. Finally, studies have revealed that touch has the capacity to communicate security – something that is in low supply for many children."[44]

This natural need often prompts teens to seek out physical connections in ways that are unhealthy. They're physically maturing and pulling away from the physical affection of parents at the same time that their eyes and mind are being inundated with fraudulent representations and images about what casual physical contact can do.

Their bodies crave touch, and culture says that touch comes from the physical act of sex, disengaging it from the relational components of real love and commitment. We're left with dangerous consequences and confusion—confusion for us, as parents, trying to explain the contradictions and, obviously, confusion for our teens as they are trying to wage their way through this complicated season of life.

So what is a parent to do? First and foremost, acknowledge the validity of your teen's physical needs. Avoid any kind of message—implicit or explicit—that touch is wrong or sinful or something to be ashamed of. Instead, acknowledge that it is natural and normal that your teen feels drawn to be close to another person. Agree that this is a tough season, full of temptations and distractions.

This is an opportunity for partnership between you and your son or daughter. When you agree that this is a tempting area that needs to be addressed, you're working with them, not against their nature. You'll earn their trust to help them set healthy boundaries, build self-control, and plan creative alternatives to avoid temptations.

Also, keep hugging them, even if they're at that awkward stage where they squirm and roll their eyes. Make eye contact when you talk, and actively listen to them with your undivided attention. Teens will be less vulnerable to artificial intimacy if they experience healthy physical affection at home.

Another way to help your teen is to recognize how they are naturally "wired" to interpret and receive affection, love, and respect. These inborn tendencies—what author Gary Chapman refers to as the five "love languages"—are words of affirmation, spending quality time together, receiving gifts, acts of service, and physical touch.[45] Different people naturally are more drawn to give and receive love in different ways, so your son or daughter's love language may not be the same as yours. If you understand what they value and respond to most, then you can offer a variety of ways to appropriately fulfill a teen's physical needs.

RECOGNIZING PHYSICAL MATURITY: OWNING THE BODY

Achieving physical maturity is easy in some ways. It happens whether we want it to or not, and at a rate that we can do little to control. The pituitary gland, located at the base of the brain, is the timekeeper for determining what will develop and when.

But the physical maturing process is also difficult because it's generally so awkward: hair is sprouting, voices are cracking, bodies are changing, skin is oily, and underarms are stinky. Hormones are all over the place.

While a teen might feel frustrated and helpless when it comes to the development of his or her body, it's important for them to realize that there is one specific aspect of physical maturity over which they have sole control: they get to choose what part of their physical body only belongs to them, what they are not "giving away" (unless abuse is a factor, as we will discuss in a later chapter). This is both their opportunity and responsibility.

For many developing teens, knowing that they have control over anything is an exciting proposition—especially when it involves something as important as sexual health. As parents, we can help them develop within this empowered area by helping them set, and commit to, healthy boundaries.

You've probably heard the saying "If you aim at nothing, you will hit it every time." If a teen doesn't set some healthy boundaries related to their sexuality, the chance of maintaining healthy sexual boundaries is slim. Setting a physical boundary is a very mature decision for a teen. A physical boundary offers a tangible goal with *relational* implications—and that automatically brings in the psychological and social dimensions of life.

PSYCHOLOGICAL

Your daughter or son's self-image is probably based on how they see themselves in their everyday environments—home, school, and any extracurricular communities. If they view themselves as accepted in their communities and worthy of respect, they will be less likely to compromise values to win the attention and respect of others. They will also be more likely to treat their own bodies with high regard and expect others to do the same. Teens with a healthy self-image are usually more responsible in the present; they realize they have a great future ahead of them.

Teens who struggle with low self-esteem or personal insecurity, on the other hand, are at greater risk for depression, anxiety, anger, eating disorders, drug and alcohol use, and unhealthy relationships. In reference to teen sex, teens may throw themselves into a relationship, hoping it will provide the security they are searching for. But another person can't "fix" their scared and lonely feelings, and they're faced with the disillusioning truth that a relationship doesn't automatically guarantee love, acceptance, respect, or security.

If they struggle with self-esteem or self-image—and most teens do at some point in their adolescence—they need your help and unconditional love. Here are a few ideas to intentionally build up your teen's self-esteem:

- Encourage them to invest themselves in something that interests them, where they have an opportunity to experience some success.

It may be sports, the arts, or academics. Be open to offbeat ideas that excite your teen, even if they don't fit your image of what you wish they would do. These skills serve as a centerpiece for strengthening their self-concept and confidence.

- Consistently talk with them about who they are and what significance they have as a human being, rather than always focusing on what they do or don't do.

- Show them how to use positive self-talk, especially at times when they might normally allow negative thoughts and feelings to take over. If you have a competitive teen who played a great soccer game but the team lost, for example, instead of saying "I'm so proud of you," change it to "You have a good reason to be proud of yourself."

- Focus on your teen's inner character and strength rather than their outward appearance and weakness. Let them know how much you value who they are and what makes your teen unique and special, rather than just what they look like.

- Try to eliminate stereotypes in your home by not allowing teasing among siblings based on looks or ability.

- Compliment them. It can be hard to remember to verbally affirm the people we see every day and in the most ordinary circumstances. But young people are looking for encouragement and validation. Tell them when they genuinely make you laugh or make a point that you hadn't considered. Thank them for taking out the trash or not taking the bait when their younger sibling tries to pick a fight. Sincere affirmations and compliments, saying thanks, and showing recognition are all ways to reinforce a teen's importance.

RECOGNIZING PSYCHOLOGICAL MATURITY: OWNING THE CONSEQUENCES

In a society that tells teens to believe "It won't happen to me" or "It's only wrong if I get caught," many kids don't seriously consider the consequences—or the benefits—of their choices. Teens who have not built the internal character traits of self-control, integrity, responsibility, respect, and courage have a tendency to act impulsively, according to peer pressure and their feelings, rather than common sense.

Therefore, one of the best signs of psychological maturity for you to look for is the ability to think through the probable consequences of options *before* making a decision: "How is this choice going to affect my day, week, year, future…even my life?"

One effective way for parents to counter this normal teen tendency of not adequately considering consequences is to implement a **cause-and-effect** environment within the home. Allowing a teen to choose, while communicating up front that every choice holds either a corresponding benefit or a corresponding consequence, is a very practical parenting approach.

To implement this kind of learning strategy, consider introducing a "stop, think, and go" approach within the home. This successful approach helps teens to make decisions based on what they **know**, rather than what they **feel**.

Here's what it looks like: let's say your son is invited to a boy/girl party on Saturday night. There is nothing blatantly against the guidelines and boundaries that you've established for your son, but something about the details of the party—or the lack of details—makes you feel uncomfortable. You do not know the family hosting the party, but you remember that their older child, now away at college, had a reputation as an instigator.

Your son really wants to go. Before you agree, encourage him to **stop** and **think** through how this choice will lead to consequences or benefits. Who will be there? Are they people who tend to make good choices? Will hanging out with them affect his reputation? What is the worst thing that might happen at this party, and how would it affect him? What is the best thing? Challenge him to think before he commits—is he truly prepared to **own** the consequences of his choice, even the worst-case scenario? How will he handle himself if things aren't what he expects?

This technique will help train the teen to process through minor life choices, which prepares them for the major life choices.

SOCIAL

As we've seen, teens are inherently relational beings. They have a natural desire to feel connected to other people, often even more than we do as adults. Their networks and communities of friends, peers, and mentors present a key role in helping them find their place as individuals, apart from the grounding sense of their families. For most teens, these shifts lead them to rely more on their peers for support than their families, at least for a time as they establish their own identities.

There are two different forms of peer pressure: positive and negative. **Positive peer pressure**, which is rarely acknowledged, is when teens encourage others to do something good. For example, a teen sees that the new kid in school is completely alone in the cafeteria. This teen says to her friends, "Let's invite the new kid to eat with us." With her encouragement, the group is more likely to reach out and treat the student like a friend too.

Compare this to **negative peer pressure**, which is the better known and probably the more common form of peer pressure. Negative peer pressure relies on excluding those who aren't acting according to the "rules." It's also called bullying and includes behaviors like:

- Shutting someone out with the "silent treatment" or other forms of ignoring
- Rough physical interaction, pushing, poking, tripping, etc.
- Sarcasm, jokes, name-calling, gossip
- Staring or mean looks
- Public ridicule, getting others to join in

Here's a parallel example to the one above: a teen sees that a new kid is eating alone in the cafeteria. She points the student out to her friends and starts to make fun of her, which leads the entire group to join in. There are likely teens in the group who are uncomfortable with the cruelty but think it's easier to follow the crowd. Going along eliminates the risk that the sarcasm and cutting words will be turned on her.

Most of the teens I meet try not to show how uncomfortable their peers make them during these difficult years. They are artificially bold

in their independence from us, their parents, and often say and do hurtful things in order to assert the independence that they aren't even sure
that they want. The home often feels like a battlefield for all parties involved, rather than a safe haven—and spending quality time together
seems nearly impossible.

This point became deeply obvious to me a few years ago when one of
our daughters went through a brief season of rebellion. She was hanging
out with the "popular" group in her high school and was pressured to be
part of an unhealthy party scene. It was all presented to her as fun and
safe...as long as they didn't get caught and for a while, she went along.
When her father and I found out and confronted her, she chose at first
to side with her friends. There were some ugly arguments in our house
for months. In our daughter's eyes, we were ruining her life, judging her
friends, and trying to keep her from growing up and having fun. But then
a few of the other teens in the group got caught doing things that were far
more serious, and they faced some major consequences. It was a wake-
up call for our daughter, who got a new perspective on the risks related
to such choices, and not long after she intentionally started seeking new
friendships.

As parents, this is where we are called to perseverance, patience, and
maturity. Our sincere efforts to meet our teens where they are during
this difficult season of life will, eventually, pay off. Teens continue to
mature, experience, and understand the social difficulties surrounding
them, and if home is still a safe place for them, eventually, most of them
begin to appreciate it again. As parents, we have to love them **through**
this stage and provide guidance, even when it's not welcomed.

- Intentionally practice some kind of regular family time: family din-
  ners, movie nights, weekend outings, weekend brunches, bike
  rides, etc. Prioritize this in your own calendar first and then engage your teen.

- Choose your battles wisely. Identify what your priorities are, and
  ensure your "fight time" is healthy and aligned accordingly. Not
  every roll of the eyes is equal.

- Think ahead about what kinds of activities your teen will automatically be allowed to do, and what must be based on earned trust. For example, are you comfortable letting them attend school sports events with their friends? Go to a friend's house to spend the night? Go to the movies without a chaperone? Get in friends' cars? If you are married, get on the same page with your spouse before a situation comes up.

- At some point, almost every kid will push the boundaries their parents have set in order to test their own independence. Accept that this will happen, and pray that your teens get caught if they are making poor choices. This may seem like odd advice, but actually, getting caught in a relatively minor offense when they're young often provides an opportunity for a crucial lesson to be learned in a safe environment and prevents them from taking even bigger risks later, when the consequences are greater.

- Intentionally allow and encourage your teen to have positive, healthy role models in their life—both men and women. Most teens have things that they want to talk about with someone other than Mom and Dad. This is natural. Coaches, mentors, church leaders, and teachers can all provide support for their growing social needs in a safe, supportive environment.

RECOGNIZING SOCIAL MATURITY: FACING PEER PRESSURE HEAD-ON

Social maturity means knowing how to respond appropriately and behave responsibly in the midst of social settings. A socially mature teen will make their own decisions regardless of the peer pressure around them.

Every young person has a desire to be liked and to be part of a peer group. Their desperate need to fit in might cause them to consider heading down a path that is not in their best interest. But they can mature and grow by learning to balance their relationships and activities, rather than investing all of their time with one person (a friend or a date). As parents, you can help by giving them opportunities to build connections and identity outside of a single setting. By getting involved in your local church, community theater, club, workplace, or sports team, the individual pressure that any one person or group can exert will be more limited.

FINANCIAL

Most teens want, at least in principle, to be adults. They can't wait to get cell phones, and drivers' licenses, and freedom. They may struggle against the idea of living under your guidelines and standards. "When I move out," more than one angry teen has said in the middle of a meltdown, "I won't have to do what you say anymore. I'll be able to do whatever I want!"

Sex and dating often get pulled into this innate desire for maturity. Sex is something "grown-up" that they can do to feel older and more in control of their lives. "I'm old enough to make my own decisions," says the boy who's considering taking things with his girlfriend to the next level. "I'm not a kid anymore."

The reality, of course, is that teens have no idea what's really involved in being an adult. Living under their parents' roof also means living under their parents' protection—and usually under their parents' financial care.

I work with teens in a variety of areas, including many school districts where families are what most people would consider "well off." The kids I meet here, to put it mildly, don't have to worry about paying a mortgage or putting food in the fridge. But that's true of most American teens. They have the freedom to focus on luxuries, like getting the "right" clothes, phones, and games, because they can trust their parents to handle the necessities.

And yet, they say they want to be adults and make their own choices.

Parents, our teens need help to realize that if they're going to engage in adult things (like sexual activity), they need to be ready to take on adult responsibilities (like taking care of themselves, and possibly another person if there's a baby). We're not doing our kids any favors by not teaching them the direct connection between poor choices, including teen sexual activity, and financial insecurity.

One of the critical lessons I share in Pure Sexual Freedom is the practical difference between surviving, thriving, and luxuries.

- **Surviving** is exactly what it sounds like: humans need food, a place to live, and basic clothing. Those things cost money.

- **Thriving** is moving past the basics, not to the point of indulging in things we *want*, but rather into things *that enhance our lives*. In a teen's life, that might mean their own bedroom, new (not hand-me-down) clothes, a car to transport them to work and school, or a basic cell phone (not a smart phone). Most teens in our current culture consider these as things that they need to *survive* everyday life, but that really is not the case. Generations of teens were just fine with a school bus and pay phones.

- **Luxuries** are the things we *want*—the designer clothes, the expensive sports lessons, and the out-of-state vacations every spring break. Many teens take these things for granted, never considering what it costs to provide.

These are concepts that can be introduced to a tween or teen at any age to help them approach adulthood more responsibly. For example, if your son says he "needs" a new video game, remind him that he doesn't *need* it; he *wants* it. Then, as they get older and you start to talk with them about boundaries within relationships and dating, they'll be prepared to understand how to consider the financial implications:

If you're ready to make adult decisions about sexual activity, are you also ready to take adult responsibility for what you need to survive and thrive?

Do you have a plan for how to provide food, clothing, and a place to live for the family that you're potentially starting (the person they're sexually active with and a child)?

I'm not saying that you should threaten to cut them off or kick them out if your teen makes a mistake. But I do think that every parent needs to have a conversation with their teen to make it crystal clear: if they choose to be sexually active, they are, in essence, making a statement that they are self-sufficient *and can support a family*. And they need to understand just how much that would cost.

I know a lot of teens who drive a car but don't have a sense for what it would take to purchase a car and pay for gas, insurance, and maintenance. I also know a lot of teens who work, but their minimum wage incomes aren't nearly enough to care for themselves, let alone an infant.

RECOGNIZING FINANCIAL MATURITY: SURVIVING THE SMART WAY

As scary as this may feel, our teens are quickly moving toward adulthood. Before they "launch," they need to be ready to face many adult things. Are they ready to demonstrate financial maturity? This includes making a budget, learning to give to help others, setting savings goals, and understanding responsible uses (and risks) of credit.

Engage with your son or daughter about financial matters early. Don't shield them from the reality of what their lifestyle costs. Encourage them to start goal-setting according to the widely used SMART technique: Specific, Measurable, Accountable, Relevant, and Timely.[1] For example, let's say your teen wants to buy a car:

- **S**pecific: Challenge your teen to set a specific financial goal for how there are going to earn money, and how much they need, based on research on the costs of different cars on the market (new, used, budget, luxury).

- **M**easurable: Provide a way for your teen to identify what is considered success. Will they save enough for a down payment or enough to buy a car outright?

- **A**ccountable: Predetermine who will hold the teen accountable. If they can't make a car payment, what will happen?

- **R**elevant: Help your teen determine what is important for their current stage of life. Do they really need the car with the fancy sunroof and souped-up engine? How much money would they save if they went with a cheaper model? Are there risks or downsides to that?

---

[1]The SMART technique often uses the words Attainable, Realistic, and Time-based. You can use whichever words best suit your desired results.

- Timely: Set a timetable for accomplishing the goal. How much do they have to save each month to get to their goal?

As they mature, they'll be able to go through this process without you and to make decisions with long-term goals in mind. The general benefit of setting SMART goals should spill over to many areas of life.

7

HELP! MY TEEN IS IN LOVE

Every now and then in my parent workshops, I get a mom or dad who asks, "My daughter's been in a committed relationship for over a year. They're inseparable, and she says she loves him. How am I supposed to counter that?"

Ah, love. It's a word that teens throw around a lot. Remember those anonymous question cards that I invite from my students? Here are the questions they ask about love:

Is there a difference between a crush and real love?

Can you have sex with someone even if you don't really love them?

Can you love someone and not have sex with them?

If you're infatuated with someone, and you know it's just infatuation, is it okay to hook up to fulfill the obsession?

Does love at first sight even exist?

Doesn't love always end with sex?

We've been friends with benefits for a while, but now I found someone I really think I might love. Do I have to tell my friends-with-benefits partner that it's over?

Where do we even start with this?

I usually start with some definitions, much to the teens' dismay—and enlightenment.

Because as hard as it is for them to admit, not every romantic feeling is love.

A **crush** is an intense feeling that comes and goes pretty quickly. Parents, you can probably remember your first crush—that boy you followed around in the hallway or that girl who you couldn't stop staring at in history class. You probably didn't really know the person, but you were obsessed with the *idea* of them, and you loved the butterfly feeling you got when you saw them. It was intense, almost physically painful...until it wasn't. You came back from Christmas break, or someone new sat at your lunchroom table, and all of a sudden you'd practically forgotten about the old flame. The crazy thing was, the new crush felt just as real and exciting as the old crush.

An **infatuation** is what happens when a crush becomes mutual. It's often still a short-lived, foolish, all-absorbing obsession...but now you can talk to the person. Infatuations spread like a virus among teenagers, who are full of emotions looking for an outlet but who are not mature enough to know how to approach a real relationship.

When someone is deeply infatuated, they cannot seem to think about anything but the source of their infatuation. It takes forever to fall asleep at night because they are busy thinking about their significant other. Their grades slip; their friends fade. One or both of them often seem to change their personalities. All the infatuated couple wants to do is be together. They've created a happily-ever-after picture about the future, where together they will make everything perfect. They get insecure or jealous easily if their infatuation talks to someone else or does not spend all of their time with them.

Typically, these unhealthy relationships don't last for long, and they usually end with someone getting hurt. Yet, in the heat of the relationship, an infatuated teen almost always calls it love.

I have spoken to probably thousands of sexually active teens over the years, and I often ask them to share their reason for having sex. Some of the most common responses are: "Well, I love her," "He said he loved me," "I thought it was no big deal because we were in love," "I wanted to show him I loved him," or "The feelings were so intense, we knew we loved each other, so it was okay."

Do you hear a common theme? They reacted to the idea of love as if it were a feeling. They're confusing physical and emotional attraction with something much deeper, and they're pushing their bodies to match what their hearts and minds definitely aren't ready for.

The English word *love* has many different meanings. It can mean affectionate, benevolent, brotherly, and of course, romantic. Contrary to what we see in the movies or read in the hyperemotional teen novels, love is not based on what one feels or doesn't feel. Love is an action. One of my favorite quotes about love comes from one of the oldest books of wisdom—the Bible:

> *"Love is patient, love is kind. It does not envy, it does not boast, it is not proud. It is not rude, it is not self-seeking, it is not easily angered, it keeps no record of wrongs. Love does not delight in evil but rejoices with the truth. It always protects, always trusts, always hopes, always perseveres."*[46]

Falling in love is a long-term *process*—it's not a physical *act*—and loving someone is a *commitment*, not a *feeling*. Love is about doing what is in the other person's best interest, and having sex as a teen is not in any teen's best interest.

So, you may ask, if infatuations are high-intensity and short-lived, and if they make my daughter or son mistake hormones for love, are they wrong? The answer is tricky. The *feelings* connected to a crush or an infatuation might not be wrong. There's nothing wrong about being attracted to another person. Dating is a normal and exciting part of growing up and sometimes matures into a healthy, long-term relationship.

Yet what a teen might choose to do sexually, based on their feelings, can potentially have devastating consequences. Mistaking infatuation for love, and then letting that become a justification for sexual activity, usually breeds a broken heart and some serious consequences. That's *not* in the best interest of anyone and is definitely dangerous.

THE DIFFERENCE BETWEEN SEX AND INTIMACY

All humans are looking for the same things: companionship, love, security, fulfillment, and intimacy. Sometimes we get confused and try to use sex to take the place of intimacy, but the two are not interchangeable. True intimacy is at the deepest level of what our teen wants as they develop into an independent adult, but—and teens hate it when I say this—it's also something that their still-developing senses of self aren't yet ready for or capable of.

Like love, intimacy is not a feeling. True intimacy—the desire to know, to be known, and to be understood in a deep way—does not happen quickly or because of a physical encounter. It's a journey, something that can only be developed over time and with a lot of trust.

Trust allows each person in an intimate relationship to feel comfortable to self-disclose and be vulnerable with each other. Without trust, it's almost impossible to have truly vulnerable, healthy interactions.

Media and culture don't talk about intimacy much, or if they do, they use it incorrectly, as a euphemism for sex. "Have you two been... intimate?" True intimacy doesn't sell like sex does. It's quiet and patient, and it challenges the attitude of instant gratification that drives our consumer-driven culture. Sex makes money. The commercial industry does not care about your daughter's self-worth or whether your son is giving in to peer pressure. It cares about keeping the malls open, about promoting the physical body as sexual "eye candy," and selling us mindless entertainment that promises happily ever after.

As parents, we are the gatekeepers against these kind of predatory messages. It's not easy, but it can be done. Rather than tuning out, or getting lost in our own screens, take the time to watch what your teen is watching. Listen to their music. Ask what they think of what they're seeing. The opportunities for conversation will arise. When you see something that promotes teen sex, ask questions. "So that seems like fun at first. But what do you think the long-term impact will be?"

The answer is invariably that "hooking up" makes things more complicated. It can create relationship ties that the teen didn't mean to make, commitments they can't back up, and emotional pain that doesn't magically disappear. Teen sex can lead to lies, secrets, guilt, and pain, not to mention children and STIs. What it doesn't lead to is true intimacy.

The dating goal for our teens during this stage of life should not be to have that feeling of butterflies and a romantic movie soundtrack. It should be to get to know more about themselves and about other people and to better understand how to relate to others. They'll learn what qualities, traits, and characteristics they like and dislike in a person. Feelings will be present, but a healthy relationship is based more on the facts than the feelings.

Healthy relationships are grounded on consistent, positive interactions, effective communication, and an emotional give-and-take that reflects health and wholeness onto both people. A healthy teen dating relationship will probably include an abundance of attraction and romantic feelings but also needs to be based on solid respect, integrity, and basic friendship.

THE ULTIMATE GOAL: HEALTHY ADULTHOOD, COMMITMENT, AND MARRIAGE

By teaching and reinforcing these ideas with your teen, you're not only helping them to avoid risky sexual behavior now, but you're also setting them up to be healthy, strong adults who are capable of lasting commitment in the form of marriage.

The focus of this book is on how you can help your *teen* son or daughter, who, statistically, is still many years away from saying "I do." At this point in your parenting, helping them choose not to engage in risky sexual activity *during the teen years* is your important challenge.

However, I want to be clear: all of the concepts covered throughout this book represent equipping teens to experience healthy dating relationships, wonderful marriages, and great sex (in that order). I believe that saving sex for the commitment of marriage is the best relationship choice for all individuals. The ultimate goal of the Pure Sexual Freedom model is to move teens in that direction.

Twenty years ago, when I first started teaching in classrooms, I spent a lot of time helping students understand why they were saving their sexual experiences for their future spouse. It was a fairly easy connection to make: I'd ask the seventh- and eighth-grade girls to tell me about their dream weddings, and most kids, including the boys, would join the conversation, or at least listen. I'd talk about their future husband or wife, and the kids would agree that they'd be married one day.

Today, that's not the case. The fourteen- and fifteen-year-olds I talk to give me blank stares when I mention marriage. Sure, every season *The Bachelor* proposes to someone, but we eventually see the tabloid headlines that report that it never lasts. Teens see twenty- and even thirty-somethings waiting to get married, relying on "hooking up" and living together to "test the waters" before settling down. A recent study shows that almost half of Millennials, now between eighteen and thirty-four, would support a marriage-like partnership that involved a two-year trial—at which point the union could be either formalized or dissolved, with no divorce or paperwork required.[47]

It's no wonder lifetime commitment just isn't part of today's adolescent vocabulary or how they see their future. Barely half of all adults in the United States are married. The average American man is almost twenty-nine when he marries for the first time, and the average American woman is almost twenty-seven. Just 20% of adults between eighteen and twenty-nine are married.[48] The divorce rate continues to frighten everyone, and many of the kids I talk to have grown up with divorced parents and/or divorced grandparents, or have friends with divorced parents.

Since you have a tween or teen living in your home, you already know what commitment is all about. It takes commitment to raise them and stay involved in their lives and their many activities! But do our sons and daughters truly understand what commitment is? Have they seen it modeled? The culture doesn't do much to show them the importance of sticking with a promise or a responsibility, regardless of the circumstances. But what are we, as parents, doing to help our children plan for long-term commitment?

If we're going to discuss the risks of teen sexual activity with our teens, we also need to talk with them about the value of marriage. After all, the vast majority (69%) of Millennials want to get married someday, and most of today's teens and tweens will follow in their footsteps.[49] So, parents, if a future marriage for your teen son or daughter is something that you value, how do we move them in that direction, during this season of life, in a healthy manner?

One key part of the Pure Sexual Freedom model is sharing with tweens and teens a vision of a healthy, happy marriage. Studies today point toward some huge benefits to marriage for children, adults, and society in general. Marriage provides:

- Healthier children

- Stronger family finances

- A longer life span

- More sex

- Safer sex

- Better sex

- Increased faithfulness[50]

Some parents have pointed out that saving sex for marriage is not a guarantee that their daughters and sons will experience intimacy, have great sex, or that sex will be easy. I completely agree. But it does guarantee that the person they fumble through it with will be someone who has already committed to love them forever.

I don't know what your current marital situation is. You may be blissfully married, not-so-happily married, divorced, widowed, or never married. You bring your own story to this conversation, and your son or daughter is one of the most important listeners who will ever hear how you feel. You are the first example they see of what an adult relationship can look like.

Are you talking to your tween or teen about what they think about marriage? About what they see and hear from the adults around them? When a family member announces that they're moving in with their partner without getting married, are you taking advantage of the opportunity to discuss the value of marriage? When you and your spouse disagree, are you explaining what healthy disagreements sound like? If you're dating, are you modeling appropriate boundaries for your teen to replicate? When a public marriage falls apart and it's all over the headlines, are you identifying the pain and hurt that the entire family is experiencing? Does your daughter or son have role models of good, healthy, committed marriages?

We can alleviate the misconceptions and fears around marriage by openly talking about them and sharing the facts. Debunking the discouraging myths about marriage and divorce might be a game-changing revelation for your daughter or son. After all, not all marriages end in divorce. A lot of marriages are happy. There are husbands and wives that are glad they married their spouse and, given the chance, would do it over again. Three of the key components to decreasing the chance of divorce and an unhappy marital life are (1) **believing the good news about marriage**, (2) **marrying the right person to begin with**, and (3) **remaining faithful to that person**. The healthy perspectives that they develop and practice in Pure Sexual Freedom will help them with those goals.

8

IS MY TEEN READY?

THE Pure Sexual Freedom model acknowledges that **teens are sexual beings and naturally desire to have sex**. We also acknowledge that teens have a choice about their sexual activity. Many parents have questioned me about that; telling our kids that they can make their own choices seems scary and maybe even irresponsible. But it's also true. Our teens are starting to make the natural progression to independence. Rules and restrictions will not prevent a determined teen from experimenting sexually if that's what they want to do.

So instead of relying on rules or threats, the Pure Sexual Freedom model works *with* teens to help them begin to understand that a healthy relationship is about far more than physical gratification or social approval. It helps them identify their own personal needs and tangibly understand their responsibilities. It shows them the consequences connected to teen promiscuity in a nonjudgmental way, while also sharing the great benefits and rewards of *not* engaging in at-risk sexual activity. More often than not, a person has to give up something in one area of life—for instance, society's definition of popularity, fun, adventure, or pleasure—to gain greater value in another area of life—such as physical, psychological, social, and financial freedom. Greater gain always has a price tag! For a teen, the price tag connected to Pure Sexual Freedom possibly involves some really hard stuff, like peer ridicule and delaying gratification.

Is your teen making the connection that the choices they make today will impact their future? Character development plays an intricate part in the choices your teen will make.

Broadly defined, character is the word we use to describe the mental and moral qualities that are unique to an individual. A person's character may be strong or weak, honest or deceptive, brave or timid. Character is the backbone to all healthy relationships. Destructive behaviors such as violence, dishonesty, drug abuse, alcohol use, and sexual promiscuity have many causes, but the absence of good character is a central one.

As parents, we won't succeed in training our teens to choose Pure Sexual Freedom if we aren't partnering our efforts with character training. Good character is not something that develops automatically; it takes intention, time, practice, and patience to help them:

- Make the right choices in difficult situations.

- Make the right choices consistently over time.

- Surround themselves with people of good character.

When we talk about teens making healthy choices regarding sexual activity, what we're really striving for is that our young people will **know** what is right and will **choose** to act accordingly. This is often referred to as a **healthy personal code of ethics**.

Pause here for a moment and consider the following statements and process through your teen's current and/or potential strengths and weaknesses. Be honest here; your teen isn't perfect, and that's not a reflection on anything you've done or haven't done. No one is perfect, and every person—especially teens with their still-developing perspectives—has things that they need to work on.

My teen:

- ☐ Shows the ability to make decisions based on what is best for both themselves and others.

- ☐ Demonstrates the willpower to do what is right even in the face of pressure.

- ☐ Thinks critically, taking all the facts into consideration when making a decision.

- [ ] Identifies and demonstrates a personal set of core values in the way that they treat people.

- [ ] Has developed and demonstrated positive habits and acts responsibly in everyday life.

- [ ] Understands that choices have either destructive consequences or constructive benefits.

- [ ] Shows remorse when they have hurt others.

- [ ] Has the ability to turn good judgment and feelings into positive actions.

- [ ] Chooses to do what is right, even when no one is looking.

There are dozens of values and attitudes that combine to create a person with good character, including compassion, fairness, honesty, and faithfulness. For the sake of this topic, let's consider five critical character traits that relate directly to teen sexual activity: **self-control, integrity, responsibility, respect, and courage**.

SELF-CONTROL

Can a teen *eliminate* his or her sexual desires? No. Can teens *control* their *actions* in reference to their sexual desires? Yes!

Will your teen control his or her actions in reference to sexual desires? Not automatically.

Self-control, broadly defined, is the basic ability to delay gratification. Like all character traits, self-control is a learned skill. Very young children learn to sit still in school or to wait for dessert until after a meal. Older children learn to control their words. This leads to the ability to control their choices, impulses, and feelings throughout their lives.

The natural desire for immediate gratification is very inviting. Teens haven't lived long enough yet to have much of a sense of the future or how fast time moves. Their temptations beckon them to feel good *now*. It's difficult for teens to realize that the temptation in front of them, which suggests a shortcut to something they deeply desire, is usually false— often leading toward something very unfulfilling and sometimes even dangerous.

People with self-control:

- Better express their feelings without being destructive.

- Do not allow their feelings to control the choices they make.

- Focus on the end result that they desire.

- Treat others with more respect.

As parents, we help our children develop and practice self-control by giving them opportunities to solve problems, exercise impulse control, set goals, look at all possibilities and consider healthy alternatives, and consider the consequences of their actions *before* they act.

Self-control doesn't mean that a teen will be able to be in the backseat of the car with their date with romantic music playing, the windows steaming up, clothes coming off, and magically not give in to sexual temptation. Actually, it's quite the opposite: a teen who has developed self-control will not put himself or herself into that situation to begin with. It's more about *preventing* themselves from getting into at-risk situations than about *intercepting* at-risk situations already in progress.

INTEGRITY

Integrity means doing what is right, simply because it's right—not because others are watching, not because it's popular or fun or cool, but because it's right. It's about behaving consistently according to your personal values.

Often, teens act in order to please their parents, their coaches, or their friends—or to avoid getting into trouble. They don't consider what they, personally, believe. And then the moment comes when they have a choice of how to act, and they are sure *no one would know*. They could cheat on the test with the answer key no one knows they have. They could take their date and park deep in the woods, where no one will see what they do.

As parents, we won't know everything our tween or teen does. It's only their integrity that will keep them safe when no one is watching.

One way to help an adolescent develop personal integrity is to simply identify it: point out acts of virtue, honesty, and respect exemplified by others and especially by your teen. Verbally acknowledge times when they display integrity, and talk with them through any decisions that you know they are facing. A personally affirmed teen will begin to experience what it feels like to be a young man or woman of integrity.

RESPONSIBILITY

Taking personal responsibility means **owning** the consequences of our actions, regardless of whether those consequences are positive or negative, easy to deal with or difficult.

The lack of responsibility leads a person to make excuses. How often have you heard "He made me do it" or "It's not my fault" or "I just wasn't thinking" or "All my friends are doing it"? The most common reaction I've heard from teen girls over the years as I sit with them in the counseling room and wait for the results of their pregnancy test is "I don't know how this happened."

When I'm talking with students, I share this list of "dating responsibilities" as a counter to all the excuses and temptations to blame others.

Teens need to know how much influence they truly have over their own lives.

I have the **responsibility**:

- To determine my own limits and values.

- To respect/not violate the limits of others.

- To communicate clearly and honestly.

- To ask for help when I need it.

- To be considerate.

- To check my actions/decisions to determine if they are good for me or bad for me.

- To set high goals for myself in my relationships.[51]

As a parent, I understand that there are times when it's difficult to allow our teens to experience consequences and watch them struggle. I've struggled to sit on my hands and hold my tongue when coaches and teachers held my daughters accountable for their behavior, and I watched them struggle with temporary disappointment and loss. But consistently rescuing our teens—often referred to as "helicopter parenting"—and not allowing natural consequences to happen might cause more harm than good down the road.

Your son or daughter is going to make mistakes somewhere in their adolescence. It's inevitable and part of growing up. It's how we learn. It's also your opportunity to help them develop that sense of responsibility that helps them take ownership of their behavior. Here are some tips for developing this critical character trait:

- Don't automatically bail your son or daughter out of difficult situations. If they don't do their homework, don't do it for them. If they get a detention for talking back to a teacher, don't call the principal to complain. Offer a listening ear and your support as they navigate the mess they've made, but don't fix it for them. It may be inconvenient, or hard to watch, but think about the long-term effects. Your daughter or son needs to learn that there are consequences to their decisions. If they think that someone else will always rescue them, it could enable destructive behavior and delay the process of maturing psychologically.

- If their peer group is getting in trouble or making poor decisions, use it as an opportunity for conversation. Talk to your tween or teen without condemnation or judgment about what role, if any, they played in the situation, and challenge them to become part of the **solution**. Ask questions like "What could you do the next time he suggests skipping school?" and "What do you think made your friends start picking on that girl?"

- Whenever your son or daughter is considering or planning a social interaction, ask them, "Who are you responsible for?" Remind them that the answer is always "myself." When his friends are going to a party where there will be drinking, or her prom date is suggesting going to an after party she thinks will be "intense," your teen needs to remember to take ownership of their own actions but not the choices that friends make. If your teen is a people-pleaser or a caretaker, they may need your help to understand they are not responsible for what their friends choose to do.

RESPECT

To show respect means to show dignity, high value, honor, and esteem. When we respect others, we deliberately refrain from hurting them.

Teens usually think of respect as something that they are supposed to show to the adults in their lives, but many of them never consider how respect factors into their peer relationships. Teens, in general, are brutal to one another. They trade insults and battle for social position and bully those who are weaker than them and generally do everything they can to build their reputations, often at the expense of others.

Disrespect is not a new problem. You probably remember the bullies in your own school; the experience often produces fear and emotional pain that is not easily forgotten.

Your teen needs to know that a person who is respectful:

- Does not intentionally injure others physically, verbally, or socially.

- Does not call others names or use sarcasm to cut them down.

- Honors what other people care about.

- Does not pressure others to do things that are not in their best interest.

Teens have the right to express their feelings when there are conflicts over differences of opinion, but often they need some assistance to learn how to do so in a respectful manner. When scenarios of conflict arise, parents are given opportunities to train our teens to choose healthy strategies for dealing with their frustration and disagreement. Here are some guidelines for establishing respectful communication in your home:

- Model healthy anger management. If you're angry, take a breath, announce that you need to take a time-out, and then walk away. Regroup when you can handle the situation calmly.

- Don't allow name-calling, threats, taunts, or other verbal abuse.

- Don't allow physical abuse: hitting, grabbing, or otherwise hurting one another.

- Help teens use words and active listening skills to express their anger: "I'm sensing you are mad or frustrated about ...," "You seem to be feeling ...," "Are you saying that ...," and "I understand this is difficult, let's discuss it some more."

- Set positive boundaries. Instead of always saying no, look for opportunities to say yes, while giving clear expectations. If the expectations are upheld, recognize that and thank your teen for being responsible. If the expectations are not upheld, implement consequences.

- Encourage healthy outlets for energy or frustration, such as exercise.

- Avoid win-lose and lose-lose situations. Power struggles are about control. The goal we're striving to reach is **training** our teens, not **controlling** them.

Apply these guidelines not just in your relationship with your teen, but model anger management in your marriage and in your relationships with others too.

It's important that teens understand that they deserve respect. They also need to know that they are responsible for respecting all of those around them—including those peers who look differently, act differently, believe differently, or otherwise aren't part of their "group." As parents, our responsibility is to teach our teens both how to give respect and expect it in return.

Consider these conversation starters to help you explore the idea of respect with your tween or teen:

- Is respecting someone a choice?

- Do you have to approve of what a person does in order to show respect?

- Do you have to like someone in order to show respect?

- What is more important to you: respect or popularity?

- Will others show you respect if you don't respect yourself?

The issues of self-respect and mutual respect become critically important when the dating stage of life begins. Consider sharing these foundational **dating rights** with your teen to ensure they have clear expectations.

In dating, every person has the right:

1. To be treated with respect always.

2. To their own body, thoughts, opinions, and property.

3. To choose and keep their own friends.

4. To change their own mind—at any time.

5. To not be abused—physically, emotionally or sexually.

6. To leave a relationship.

7. To say no.

8. To be treated as an equal.

9. To disagree.

10. To live without fear and confusion from their boyfriend's or girl-friend's anger.[52]

If your teen finds themselves in a relationship where any of these rights are violated, it's a red flag that the connection is deeply unhealthy and the relationship should probably end.

COURAGE

Martin Luther King, Jr. famously said, "The ultimate measure of a man is not where he stands in moments of comfort and convenience, but where he stands at times of challenge and controversy."

Courage is having the fortitude and strength to publicly act on behalf of your beliefs, even when it's hard. It's one thing to **know** what is right, but having the courage to publicly do what is right, even in the face of disapproval or ridicule, is an entirely different concept.

Courage doesn't necessarily mean jumping on the cafeteria table and denouncing what is wrong. Often it means publicly living out one's integrity. When one of our daughters was a junior in high school, she was invited to an unsupervised Halloween party where there would be a lot of drinking. The rumor was that most of the school would be there that night. Instead of going along or making up some excuse, our daughter chose to plan her own alternative event. She invited a bunch of her friends to come to our house for a night of silly costumes, trick-or-treating, and Chinese food. Some of her classmates made fun of her "good girl plan"—or at least they did until she and her friends had a blast that night, and the other party got broken up by the cops.

Fear often plays a huge role in whether or not your teen will be capable of standing up for what they know is right. Whether they admit it or not, most teens are afraid of something. Do you know what that is for your son or daughter?

Take an honest look at your teen. Start some conversations. How do they feel about:

• Failure?

- Standing alone?

- Trusting others?

- Life without love?

- Losing a relationship (romantic or friendship)?

- Being mocked?

- Peer pressure?

- Being "different"?

Pay attention to your teen. If it seems like they're pulling away from their friends or withdrawing from the family, take the time to find out why. They may be facing a specific situation where they need your help.

When you're helping your daughter or son build courage, be sure to share your positive impressions. Don't doubt them. Let them know you believe in them and know they can make healthy choices. Your teen needs to know that no matter what happens, you will support their efforts to be courageous in making healthy choices.

MATURITY AND THE PURE SEXUAL FREEDOM MODEL

As character develops, so does maturity—a person's growth to full, adult experience and perspective.

Tim Elmore, president of the nonprofit group Growing Leaders, looks for these characteristics of maturity in teens and young adults:

- A mature person is able to keep long-term commitments.

- A mature person is unshaken by flattery or criticism.

- A mature person possesses a spirit of humility.

- A mature person's decisions are based on character not feelings.

- A mature person expresses gratitude consistently.

- A mature person knows how to prioritize others before themselves.

- A mature person seeks wisdom before acting.[53]

As your teen matures and develops their character, you will see these aspects of maturity demonstrate themselves in each part of the Pure Sexual Freedom model.

- **Physical**: Their physical bodies are healthy, free of unplanned pregnancy and devastating infections or diseases.

- **Psychological**: They are able to concentrate on enjoying life as teens when their minds and emotions are free from painful memories and lost dreams that often accompany teen sex and broken relationships. They can learn more about who they are as an individual and better determine what they want out of life.

- **Social**: Their social environments remain spontaneous and unhindered by the complications of sexual activity. Their social life is not controlled by one individual or relationship. There is no guilt, fear, or condemnation. Also, their peer social group can be natural and normal, instead of fake and stressful.

- **Financial**: They won't be worried about necessities for survival but will be conscious and responsible about how items that enhance their lives (or even add some luxuries) are prioritized. They will know how to set long-term goals and will focus on the future.

PART 4: SETTING BOUNDARIES THAT STICK

Noel's story:

When I was nineteen years old, I found out that I was pregnant. The medical pregnancy clinic that gave me my pregnancy verification educated me about my options. I went over my options again and again, but within a few weeks, I knew that I wanted to place my child for adoption.

After meeting with the advisors at three different adoption placement agencies, I decided which agency I was most comfortable with and started the placement process. I received a call from the family I'd selected, and since we were fortunate to live in the same city, I met them at a restaurant for lunch, and they shared their story. They had been trying to have a child for eight years and had experienced several miscarriages and unsuccessful infertility procedures. Here I was, emotionally distraught because I was pregnant, and they were emotionally burdened because they weren't pregnant. It gave me a totally different view of adoption. I was six months pregnant then, and for the rest of my pregnancy, we saw each other almost weekly. The adoptive mother threw a party for my birthday, and I got to meet most of their friends.

When I went into labor a week early, the adoptive mother was the first person I called. My son's adoptive parents waited for him in the nursery. He was never alone. During my stay in the hospital, the adoptive mother stayed in the room with me. We stayed up all night the first night and talked. I felt like a young girl at a slumber party.

That was the beginning of a truly amazing relationship. I see them occasionally, and every time it is like seeing an old friend. I am drastically comforted by seeing how happy my son is and how wonderful his life is.

9

SETTING BOUNDARIES EARLY

Wᴇ'ᴠᴇ spent the first half of the book discussing the principles and guiding ideas behind the Pure Sexual Freedom model. Now it's time to get more practical: what can you, as parents, do to help guide your tween and teen through these challenging years?

The opportunities start long before they have their first boyfriend or girlfriend —and ideally even before they express an interest in dating. There's no perfect age to start having conversations about dating, but as your daughter or son reaches puberty, you can begin to create the framework of boundaries on which they will base their future decisions. By the time they are old enough to be in truly risky situations, they'll have the self-awareness and self-respect to be able to face what the culture throws at them.

Just to warn you in advance, many tweens and teens don't instinctively see the need for boundaries. They may roll their eyes and tell you that you're "making a big deal out of nothing." They'll feel that boundaries are just restrictions put in place to make sure they don't have fun. But most of the time, just the opposite is true. Boundaries actually provide our kids with unbelievable freedom to become who they want to become without the burden of life-changing hardships.

Consider this analogy: When our children are young, we teach them to "stop, drop, and roll" if they catch on fire. Can you imagine telling your kids to "stop, drop, and roll—*if you feel like it*?" We also tell our kids, "Don't talk to strangers." Would you consider saying, "Don't talk to strangers *unless everyone else is doing it?*" Another common one is "Look both ways when you cross the street." Would any parent ever say, "Look both ways *unless your friends will make fun of you?*"

When our kids are young, we boldly and automatically set boundaries. We do it for their safety, because we love them and know what is in their best interest. So the question becomes, why do we stop when our kids enter middle school and high school? Yes, their bodies are changing, and they're developing their own independence. It's an awkward time. But they're still curious about things that could hurt them. They are surrounded by unhealthy influences. And even in middle school, they're probably exposed to friends who are sexually active. Teens without firm boundaries, who are forced to bear the weight of responsibility for what they should do and where they should be, often choose at-risk behavior.

We are the parents. Not their BFFs, not the "cool mom," not the most popular dad ...the parents! Let's not minimize the importance of parental boundary setting out of fear.

Teens may not like the idea of boundaries on the surface, but at a deeper level, they intuitively feel uneasiness when there are no guidelines in place. One public health study among adolescents in the United States discovered that teens desire structure. "Too many kids—rich and poor—are left to their own devices."[54] Too much freedom or responsibility often leads to an intense feeling of insecurity when it's coupled with immaturity, which is why established boundary setting in advance is imperative to a teen's level of confidence.

IS YOUR TEEN A LEADER OR A FOLLOWER?

All peer groups consist of leaders and followers. So as you start to prepare your tween or teen to handle the temptations and pressures of common teen social settings, ask yourself honestly which direction they naturally gravitate toward. Some teens easily take the lead. Other teens automatically sit back, observe, and follow. There's no right or wrong answer, and one is not better or worse than another.

How often one leads versus follows is based on **temperament**. A person's temperament is the set of their mental, physical, and emotional traits—it's their natural predisposition for how they think, act, and feel. Regardless of what your teen naturally chooses, they need to understand that both roles have responsibilities. A **leader** needs to make good choices because others **will** follow them, and a **follower** must choose good, solid leaders to reduce the potential for risky situations.

If your teen is naturally a leader, help them consider how their example can influence others in a group—either in constructive or destructive ways. If your teen is a follower, help them acknowledge this and identify ways to strengthen their internal focus and fortitude when dealing with external social pressure.

PERSONAL SPACE AND TEEN RELATIONSHIPS

One of the most important ways for adolescents to prepare for healthy relationships is to establish and own their own physical and emotional "safe personal space." We can help our kids when they're as young as fifth and sixth grades to understand the boundaries of how much they are willing to share with others and what truly only belongs to them alone. The more they understand this now, the easier it will be to hold to those principles later, when attraction and hormones are involved.

Most tweens don't have the discernment to process through this a-lone or to define their boundaries when they're making friends. Look for opportunities to start conversations and partner with them to provide some guidance. Start by asking questions.

Do your friends:

- Take your stuff without asking?

- Tease and make fun of you?

- Share your private information with others?

- Act like it's your responsibility to make sure they are happy?

- Respect you and leave you alone when you say "no"?

- Honor your need for privacy when you request it?

- Give unhealthy advice or suggest doing things that you know you shouldn't do?

- Criticize you more than encourage?

- Withdraw or make fun of you when you make a good decision?

Learning to establish a safe personal space lays the foundation for a young person to know what they are comfortable and uncomfortable with in various situations. If your daughter or son learns to consider their friends this way when they're young, those boundaries will natu-rally carry forward into dating relationships.

If your tween or young teenager finds themselves in a situation where they're uncomfortable because of the behavior of a classmate or friend, talk to them about what made them feel uncomfortable.

- Who was involved?

- What was the environment?

- Why do you think you felt uncomfortable—what was "off" about it?

- What can you do in the future to have a different outcome?

Your tween's responses to these types of questions can help them see whether they need to reconsider particular friendships, and it will teach you a lot about how they uniquely handle peer pressure, friendships, and other relationships that may become risky in the future.

Unhealthy scenarios usually have a **common denominator**, which may be a particular type of person or situation. Every person is different in this regard. Is your son always getting into trouble when he hangs out with a particular friend? Is your daughter easily swayed by the girls she thinks are cooler than she is? Does he have a pattern of lying to authorities to stay out of trouble? Try to help them identify their own common denominators, and then discuss what they can do to improve or avoid such situations.

By creating a pattern of open dialogue with your children when they're young and more open to sharing, you'll also establish patterns that will help you as they get older, when the natural hormonal tendency is to want Mom and Dad to stay out of their personal business.

SEXY VERSUS MODEST

If you look at the commercials on TV and the billboards on the highway, America's definitions of "beautiful" and "handsome" equate to "hot" and "sexy."

Reality TV brings us five-year-olds in full makeup and crop tops, and tweens competing for recording contracts by belting out songs with lyrics meant for adults three times their age. Department stores carry thong underwear for elementary school girls. Video games for middle schoolers feature scantily clad characters with curves well beyond what a sixth-grade boy sees on the playground. T-shirts carry graphic and suggestive text. Celebrities on magazine covers are Photoshopped. And don't even get me started on the "sexy" Halloween costumes in elementary school parades.

Teens are used to being exposed to all body parts and to seeing private acts in public places and sexual activity being promoted as a form of entertainment.

The way children dress now is way out of line with a preteen's cognitive and emotional development, regardless of what their body might look like. Girls and boys are drawn to these adult images, even as the unobtainable standards undermine their confidence in their own bodies and their respect for the real people around them. Studies show that 50% of girls eleven to thirteen see themselves as overweight and 80% of thirteen-year-olds have attempted to lose weight.[55]

That negative self-image carries forward into high school and makes girls more vulnerable to seeking unhealthy attention and affirmation, making them more vulnerable to sexual experimentation.

The lack of modesty in our country is a real problem, and one where the double standard of how we treat girls and boys is once again clearly evidenced.

Let me be clear: the female body is beautiful and good. The female body is not the problem. Nor is this an issue because boys who see some skin "can't help themselves" in how they react. Our sons are capable of self-control and respect, and we should expect this in their behavior.

However, we live in a world where it's easy to distort the beauty and goodness of the female body for commercial gain.

There are many examples of ways our culture objectifies the female body, divorcing it from the female person and disorienting it from its proper purpose, which is relationship with others. It is not possible to have a relationship with an object. As simple as this sounds, tweens and teens—both boys and girls—who are surrounded by idealized objects need to be led to respect the female body as a person, not just a body.

But it's a complicated topic. When hackers steal celebrities' photos and share them with the public, we all agree that the invasion of privacy is unacceptable and needs to be dealt with. But it also brings up questions about the photos themselves. When the celebrities allowed themselves to be photographed nude, was it objectification or empowerment? When a female musician performs onstage wearing next to nothing and moves in sexually suggestive ways, can we later complain when fans and reviewers don't take her seriously?

When women flaunt their bodies, they are damaging the very mes-sages of empowerment and equality that they claim to champion. And our young sons and daughters are watching every minute of it, confused.

When girls flaunt their bodies with short skirts and heavy makeup, they're seeking attention for how they look, not who they are. They're trying to live up to an impossible standard that they've been given: you're only as good as you look, and you only look good if you look sexy.

Fashions come and go. Skirt hems and necklines go up and down; pants droop to uncomfortable depths. Clothing gets tight in some sea-sons and baggy in others. But modesty is always an option.

When we talk about modesty, I don't mean that our children should wear turtleneck shirts and skirts below their knees. I don't think we need to instill a list of dos and don'ts. It's not about feeling ashamed of our bod-ies. Instead, it's about self-respect! It's about taking that "safe personal space" concept that we've applied to relationships and also applying it to our bodies. What belongs to your daughter and to her alone?

Consider these suggestions as you approach this conversation with your teen:

- Consistently emphasize that your teen is not just the sum of their physical parts.

- Explain that wearing clothing that does not appropriately cover private body parts can send the wrong message and cause disre-spect, even if that's not your teen's intention.

- Reinforce to both your sons and daughters that celebrities and other people in the news are individuals with feelings and minds and are more than objects. Demystify the effects by talking about what a person's motivation might be for wearing certain clothing or acting in certain ways.

- Shop together as a family. Doing so during the tween years allows open dialogue about what is appropriate and why certain fashion statements are inappropriate. Talk about what you see in stores. Ask questions. *What makes that inappropriate? How would you feel if you were wearing that outfit?*

- Talk to your son or daughter about who they are as a person more than you talk about what they look like or what they're wearing.

- Model good clothing choices by wearing modest, fashionable clothing in front of your teen. Demonstrate the fact that you can look good at any age without flaunting yourself.

- Discuss the cycle of fads. Popular styles will come and go very quickly. Identify this so your teen will begin to understand the purpose behind marketing trends.

- If your daughter or son is uncomfortable undressing in front of others in locker rooms or other situations, respect their natural desire for modesty, and help them think about alternatives. Let them know that you'll support them and provide a safety net when they feel uncomfortable, and let them know it's appropriate to request privacy.

- Promote respect for modesty in your home. Respect your adolescent's need for physical privacy as they dress.

INNOCENT FLIRTING VERSUS SEXUAL FOREPLAY

Have you gone to a mall on a Friday night recently? It's full of teens and young adults in full displays of public affection. I've seen teen girls, wearing very little clothing, sitting on boys' laps in front of Victoria's Secret stores, surrounded by images of women wearing even less. I've seen kids in my sexual health classes give each other back rubs that touch all sorts of areas that are extremely close to the underwear zone. I've seen boys blatantly look a girl head to toe—and everything in between—before making a suggestive compliment.

And if they're doing this in public, what's happening in private?

When I talk to students about it, they consistently roll their eyes and say, "It's no big deal." They don't see themselves as being sexual at all. The images around our tweens and teens are so full of personal contact, it's no wonder that our teens no longer have the ability to recognize what is appropriate and healthy.

Here's a list of examples I use with my students to help them distinguish the difference between what's acceptable—innocent flirting—and what can only be considered sexual foreplay. Students usually hate it, because it draws out the inconsistencies in their behavior. Use this list as a springboard to start a conversation with your own tween or teen to help them see where lines can be crossed, even unintentionally.

Appropriate:

- Making innocent eye contact

- Writing cute, sweet notes

- Surprising each other

- Having inside jokes

- Sharing smiles and looks just for that person

- Dressing cutely, attractively, and modestly

- Hugging

- Holding hands

- Giving creative gifts

- Dating

Inappropriate:

- Undressing one another with your eyes

- Sexting and giving each other inappropriate photos

- Lying down together to watch a romantic movie

- Taking naps together

- Back massages

- Removing clothing or trying on clothing together

- Hanging out in bedrooms

- Hanging out behind closed doors

- Making out in a car

While it may feel uncomfortable, talk to your son or daughter about how they will handle a situation where someone else's behavior is crossing the line. What should your son do if one of his female friends unexpectedly sits on his lap? What should your daughter do if a boy on the bus coming home from a sports game starts rubbing her back suggestively?

Our tweens and teens need our help to reset the "default" of their own acceptable behavior and to know how to deal with others who may not live by the same standards. You need to be blunt and consistent to help them understand that their interactions should not be about turning one another into bodies or trying to sexually turn each other on, but to truly get to know one another.

Positive behavior creates solid friendships; it doesn't initiate sexual foreplay. Keeping their behavior respectful of each person's "safe space":

- Provides a way to truly get to know each other.

- Increases self-respect.

- Increases respect from others.

- Gives a clear conscience and peace of mind about the future.

- Offers a chance to pursue individual goals.

- Moves one closer to finding—and being—The One.

- Prevents later comparisons in marriage.

- Teaches them to treat others as complete human beings, not just bodies.

- Allows one to be loved for WHO they are rather than WHAT they do.

"Dialing down" to modesty and innocent flirting are specific areas where boundary setting makes a difference.

HOW TO SET HEALTHY BOUNDARIES

As we process through the importance of boundary setting, we begin to realize that our kids won't live under our roofs forever. We might be the most incredible parents who have ever walked on the face of this earth, but our kids will leave our homes someday. Parents can't fix everything and can't control everything. But if we consistently set boundaries early and keep the lines of communication and respect open through the teen years, we can prepare our kids to set and honor their own boundaries when we're not around.

Here are some guidelines for setting boundaries, whether they're about what your tween or teen wears, how they act in public, or how they handle sexual pressure later:

1. **Identify the potential risks.** Help your teen develop common sense about how to handle peer pressure situations. Identify the potential risks of common scenarios like unchaperoned boy-girl parties, alcohol and drugs, sleepovers with friends who are eager to experiment or rebel, public displays of affection, and bullying. If a young person finds themselves in a vulnerable situation and hasn't thought through a scenario, the desire to fit in or innocent ignorance might lead to a disastrous outcome.

2. **Set the boundary.** Once the potential risks have been identified, help your teen set an appropriate boundary. Communicate early and often about what is healthy and safe and what is not. If your son or daughter has a boundary set well in advance of an unhealthy or unsafe option, they are less likely to impulsively make a poor choice.

3. **Communicate the boundaries to others.** Now that the standards have been set and the potential risks have been identified, teach your son or daughter how to communicate their boundaries to their peers and protect themselves. Teens will not automatically wake up and know how to say "no." Instead, they need to rehearse responses within the safety of the home. Doing so will provide them with the confidence they need to stand up for what they know is in their best interest.

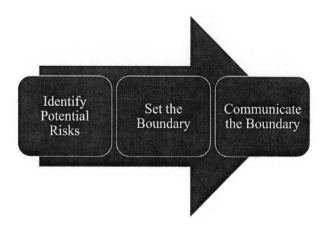

Assertiveness isn't always a word that we think we want to see in our tweens and teens. However, **healthy assertiveness** can be one of their most valuable assets in handling temptations.

Healthy assertiveness flows out of your teen's personal confidence and results in them making a choice, having an opinion, and independently deciding their actions regardless of what others do. It's tough to be, or seem to be, the only teen who says "no." But it can be done!

Here are some all-too-common statements that teens use to pressure each other into engaging in sexual activity. Share these peer pressure statements and their responses with your teen son or daughter long before you think they'll need them:

- **If you love me, you'll prove it.** *If you love me, you will choose to do what's best for me.*

- **It's safe. We can use birth control.** *No birth control provides 100% protection.*

- **Everybody else is doing it.** *Well, I guess it will be easy for you to find someone else then.*

- **Don't be a tease; we've already done…we might as well do more.** *Don't be stupid; my past doesn't control my future.*

- **I know you want to.** *No, you want me to, even if it means hurting me.*

- **It's just part of growing up.** *No, acne is part of growing up. My/your belly growing due to pregnancy is not part of growing up.*

- **I thought you loved me!** *I thought you respected me!*

Your teen will probably think this is kind of silly. But don't discount the importance of role playing. Encourage them to come up with their own responses to these suggestions. This form of prep time and practicing will help the teen identify peer pressure and will give the teen a sense of comfort and courage to respond to the peer pressure.

JUST SAY NO

In addition to encouraging your teen's assertiveness skills, it's also wise to help them learn as many ways as possible to say no. "No" is not just a word. It's an attitude, a force to be reckoned with. With practice, their "no" can be both definite and still respectful. They don't need to be seen as judging their peers; they just need to not get pulled into behavior that can harm them.

Here are some creative refusal skills to intentionally equip our teens for the realities they will face. Encourage your teen to find ones that fit their personality and style.

- **Just say no.** *No. No way. I'll pass. Not. Forget it. Count me out. Never.*

- **Ignore.** Pretend to be busy, listen to someone else, or look like you're just not paying attention.

- **Make an excuse.** *I've got to finish my homework. My parents would ground me big time. I've got _____ practice.*

- **Change the subject.** *What are you wearing to the dance on Friday? Did you watch the game Sunday night?*

- **Make a joke.** *Are you kidding? If I did that, my reputation might improve. I never do that on the days that end in y.*

- **Use flattery.** *You're too smart to mean that. You always think of great ideas, think of one now. You're too good of a friend for me to let you do that.*

- **Act shocked.** *Are you crazy? Earth calling _____. I'm gonna act like you didn't say that. Do you know how much trouble we would get into?*

- **Suggest an alternative.** *I've got a better idea! Let's _____ instead. Why don't we _____ instead?*

- **Leave!**

- **Use a code word system.** Call or text a parent and let them know you need assistance. (See the next section for more info.)

- **Return the challenge.** *If you were my friend, you would get off my back. Friends don't pressure friends.*

CREATING A CODE WORD SYSTEM

Before our teens move into the stage where they are spending time alone with friends, it's important to let them know that we are prepared to support them if they are pressured to make poor choices.

As a practical tool, consider implementing a **code word** agreement in your home. This means that if your teen contacts you and says or texts a predetermined word or phrase, you agree to immediately come to his or her aid. Promise to honor your teen's relationships and responsible choices by not doing anything to punish or turn in the friends involved (unless it's a life-and-death situation), and promise that there will be **no questions asked** until the next day, when you can sit down and discuss the situation calmly.

This form of agreement provides our teens with an "out" when they need help. They can use us as the excuse for why they need to leave a situation abruptly or not participate in a social setting that makes them uncomfortable. When we guarantee our support like this, it confirms that we are aware of the difficulties related to our daughter or son's peer environment and that we will back them when they choose to respond in a healthy, socially mature manner.

10

DATING: SAFELY PLAYING THE GAME

TELEVISION has turned dating into a game. I'm not just talking about the old dating game TV show that was popular when we were growing up. I'm talking about the plethora of popular "reality" dating shows that fill prime-time TV and lead young people to think of dating as something to be "won," with sex, love, and relationships—in that order—as the trophies.

Of course, once the cameras turn off we don't see what really happens to those "happy" couples. Instead, we see that when teens play the dating game based on unhealthy choices, the "winners" often end up feeling like they've been played.

Our teens are inundated with songs, movies, and advice that contradicts a healthy design for love and intimacy. Their already-heightened emotions rise and fall with a simple glance, touch, kiss, or word.

As parents we have an opportunity to go against this cultural sway. Some parents will do so by helping their teens reject the idea of modern dating completely, while others will look for ways to offer counterintuitive ideas for spending time with a special person. Every family needs to make their own decisions regarding dating, and to communicate those early and clearly to your children, so that the expectations are clear. The next few pages will explore how parents who have decided that they are okay with their son or daughter dating can approach it in a way that encourages positive, healthy behavior.

WHEN YOUR TEEN WANTS TO DATE

Hopefully, you and your teen have already discussed your established house guidelines for dating. If not, the time is now! It's wise to do so long before they tell you that they'd like to spend more time with a special someone. Assuming those guidelines are met—ether your teen has reached the agreed-on age or level of maturity—then it's time to talk about specifics.

Let your teen know that no matter how old they are, and no matter how many dates they go on, they should always be prepared to answer a few general questions:

- **Who** are they going out with?

- **What** are they going to do on the date?

- **Where** are they going to go?

- **Why** are they dating this individual?

- **How** will they communicate their goal of Pure Sexual Freedom to their date in this situation?

In our house, we've added another question: When will we, as the parents, meet the date? For us, it's important that we have a conversation with a young man before he leaves with our daughter. However, for some of the families I counsel, I know this isn't logistically possible, or it's less of a priority for them. If your teen is the one going to pick up their date or they're meeting in a public place under the umbrella of another chaperone or group, you may not have a chance to meet the object of their affections right away. Like everything, this is something for you to work out within your family, finding the boundaries that are most appropriate for your child. There is no "right" list of boundaries and guidelines that are guaranteed to protect every child.

Once the initial questions are addressed to your satisfaction, remind your teen of a few simple facts that frame any dating relationship and provide perspective:

- The person they are dating is someone's son or daughter.

- The person they are dating is someone's future spouse.

- They are someone's future spouse.

- This dating relationship will lay a foundation for their future dating relationships.

And, to simplify even more, use this easy-to-remember teaching method, often referred to as the "**The 3 Alls, the 3 Anys, and the 3 Avoids**":

- Keep **all** your clothes, **all** the way on, **all** the time.

- Don't let **any** part of **any**one else's body get **any**where in between you and your clothes.

- **Avoid** arousal, **avoid** tempting environments, and **avoid** domineering relationships.

Talking to your teen at this level of detail may make them blush. In my experience, most kids don't have an ulterior motive or a lot of false charm when the dating stage of life begins. It's a scary and exciting time, and usually they're too distracted hoping they won't trip in front of their date or say something too embarrassing to think much about the bigger scale of things. But the more you reinforce the thoughts, your teen's healthy awareness is heightened.

CREATIVE DATE IDEAS

It's important to make sure that when you talk to your teen about dating, you don't always focus on the dangers or negative possibilities. Dating is supposed to be a fun, enjoyable activity in a teen's life. Support that by helping them plan fun, creative ways to spend time with a person who interests them.

Here are some ideas to help you get started:

- Playing miniature golf

- Ice skating

- Fishing

- Going to an amusement park

- Flying kites

- Baking cookies

- Biking

- Double dating, group dates

- Cooking a meal for friends or family

- Going to a concert

- Creating a scavenger hunt for a younger sibling or friend

- Playing ping pong

- Completing a puzzle together

- Playing air hockey or arcade games

- Going to a sporting event

- Bowling

- Throwing a Frisbee or playing Frisbee golf

- Jogging/walking

- Taking the family pet for a walk

- Hanging out at a coffee shop

- Running errands for the family

- Volunteering at a homeless shelter or a nursing home

- Volunteering at the nearest pet shelter

- Attending youth group or church activities together

- Working out together at the local fitness gym

- Organizing a progressive dinner for friends, where they go to one restaurant for appetizers, another one for dinner, and a third one for dessert

The suggestions listed are not the normal dates that teens are currently planning. Teens tend to play video games, watch TV, go to the movies, or "hang out" with their peers. Yet these kinds of activities don't encourage them to actually interact with one another, or they open the door for all sorts of temptations.

Helping your teen try "old-fashioned" dating won't prevent them from sexual activity if they're determined to try, but it will give them healthy alternatives that will limit the time they're alone or exposed to possible temptation. Not only will the teens have fun, but they'll also learn more about themselves, their dates, and what they're looking for in the future.

THE DECEPTIONS OF DATING

Parents sometimes ask why I suggest that they ask why their son or daughter wants to date an individual. I tell them that many teens approach dating for all the wrong reasons, which increases the chances that they will end up making costly mistakes along the way. Here are three dating deceptions to look for and guidelines for how to help teens navigate past the wrong ideas.

1. "FINDING THE ONE"

Teens everywhere—especially those who are already struggling with self-esteem issues—have fallen for the Hollywood lie that there is one person in the world who holds the key to their future happiness. "You complete me" isn't just a popular line from an old romantic comedy; it's the genuine hope of many anxious teenagers today who think that as soon as they find the right person, all of their dreams will come true, their problems will disappear, and they'll live happily ever after.

Desperate to find The One, these teens date everyone they can, moving toward dangerous signs of codependency. Their sense of validation or security starts to come from somebody else, and the story typically goes in one of two ways:

- The teen begins dating a person and loses the ability to think defensively. They believe this person must be The One, even if all the evidence points against it.

- The teen dates over and over and eventually gets so used and abused that they give up on finding The One. They may start to think that they deserve constant disappointment.

If your daughter or son is approaching dating as a way to complete themselves or with the dream of one, perfect person, it's time to step in with a dose of reality.

The truth is that no single man or woman will ever meet all of our teen's needs, not even the person they eventually commit to for life. The key to happiness and contentment during these early dating years is to develop as a complete individual and to focus on **becoming** the right person instead of **finding** the right person.

If teens use this strategy, chances are they will *eventually* find the right person, though statistically it will probably happen long past the teen years, when they are more aware of who they are and what kind of future and spouse they're actually looking for.

2. "CHANGES"

There are two different sides to this same deception.

We see the first side—"I'll change"—in the teen who seems to become a different person overnight. You may no longer recognize what they like, what they don't like, how they dress, how they act, their values, their goals…even who they are. They no longer spend time with their old friends, and they drop their old activities. They parrot the opinions of the person they're dating, probably because they are so consumed with being liked or feeling loved that they've lost track of what's most important to them.

Teens who are disappearing into another person are often surrounded by others who can see the red flags, but it takes time—and often heartbreak—before the teen is willing to listen to anyone around them, even the people who know them well and sincerely love them.

The other side of the coin could be called "I'll change them." This is sometimes also called "missionary dating" because it pairs two people together who have different beliefs, values, habits, or lifestyles. One teen stays in the relationship despite the challenges, and often the unhealthy pressures, because they feel like they can "help" the other person, or even "save" them. Although many teens enter these relationships with good intentions, there's also a bit of a savior complex involved.

In both cases of "change" dating, what your teen needs is help to recognize that being in a relationship should not, and usually does not, fundamentally change an individual. Relationships are about compromise and learning to negotiate and communicate with the other person, not about changing them or changing who you are. If someone truly values your teen as a person, they will honor and appreciate them for who they are, complete with likes and dislikes, quirks, values, hopes, and dreams for the future. And if your teen truly values someone else, they will recognize that they can't change them—and quite probably shouldn't be dating them.

A teen is not responsible for changing another person, including their boyfriend or girlfriend. Healthy teens have enough to do working on their own personal desires, talents, and abilities rather than trying to lead another individual to do the same.

3. "HOOKING UP"

Your teen may not want to admit to you that this is their purpose in dating, but that doesn't mean it isn't happening. "Hooking up" dating is one of the most concerning trends affecting young people today. Guys and girls are agreeing (in spoken or unspoken terms) to engage in sexual activity with an understanding that there are no expectations in place. They don't have to agree on a level of commitment or define the relationship. The hooking up game is sugarcoated as a win/win situation for both participants and is heavily promoted in popular movies and TV shows.

This concept is difficult to understand for many parents, let alone confront. Even if your own teen activity involved a lot of casual making out or even sex, it seems different when it's our own kids who are testing their boundaries just for the sake of the experience and cultural acceptance. It's natural to want to protect your son or daughter's heart and reputation, and that starts with making sure that your messages about Pure Sexual Freedom are consistent and clear. Even if it's uncomfortable, talk to your son or daughter about how their sexuality is worth respecting and protecting.

They may think they're hooking up with no strings attached, but there are consequences:

- Jealousy will inevitably take over.

- At some point, one partner or the other will be hurt or offended by the other person's lack of love and devotion.

- It will feel lonely.

- It's hard on a person's self-esteem to feel like the other person doesn't want to be connected to their mind and heart, as well as their body.

- It's inevitable that one person will develop stronger emotions for the other and ultimately want more out of the relationship.

- The selfish foundation will poison everything. Good relationships come from giving, but hooking up is all about taking.

- It distracts both people's ability to develop healthier, more fulfilling relationships. What happens if "The One" comes along?

Explain that sex is a good thing within proper contexts. It was created to deepen the love within a marital relationship, and hooking up with someone cheapens that.

SMART DATING VERSUS STUPID DATING

Due to the number of misconceptions and poor examples of dating that teens live with today, I implemented a simple activity with students in the classroom to identify what I call "smart dating" versus "stupid dating." Obviously, there are more examples than the ones I'm sharing, but this list can help you initiate a conversation with your teen.

SMART DATING:

- Being selective

- Being specific about making your dating environment fun, creative, and safe

- Being able to communicate through the natural highs and lows of a relationship in a healthy manner

- Only dating someone with common goals and values

- Making friendship and common interests the foundation of the relationship

- Setting standards up front, communicating standards, and sticking to standards

- Spending time with other friends

STUPID DATING:

- Dating someone because they're cute, popular, or breathing

- Seeing each other only one-on-one, in secluded places

- Using the silent treatment, shouting, gossiping, sending angry texts, or posting nasty messages on social media

- Dating in order to change someone

- Basing the relationship on a physical foundation

- Getting together to "just hang out and see what happens" or choosing to hang out in environments that promote high-risk activity

- Only spending time with one another to the exclusion of other friends

DATING RED FLAGS

Fueled by impulsiveness, hormones, and a general lack of maturity, teen dating relationships can turn unhealthy quickly, and a teen who doesn't have much experience with dating or relationships is often not in the best position to recognize the warning signs.

Before they start dating, talk to your teen about attitudes and actions to look for, and watch their budding relationships carefully for any red flags such as:

- **Jealousy and possessiveness.** Exhibiting feelings of paranoia or ownership over another person. Trying to prevent them from engaging with other people or activities.

- **Insecurity.** Consistently asking for reassurance or pushing the buttons of another person's insecurities to feel better about themselves.

- **Anger.** Shouting or the silent treatment, often used to intimidate or pressure a date to comply or appease.

- **Intimidation.** Threatening someone, and then often laughing it off as a joke. Creating a sense of threat—sometimes subtle, sometimes explicit—to coerce another into appeasing the intimidator, even if it means doing things that make the doer uncomfortable.

- **Accusations.** Unreasonably charging someone with doing or feeling negative things in order to get the other person to change their behavior.

- **Flattery.** Throwing excessive compliments around as a way to win attention or behavior.

- **Status.** Showing off a position that is honored or respected (a start athlete, a popular band, a leadership role at church) in order to attract attention.

- **Bribery.** Buying gifts for their boyfriend/girlfriend with high expectations of what they deserve to get in return.

- **Consensual humiliation and abuse.** Presenting the idea that humiliation and abuse, physical or emotional, is okay and even romantic because with love and support, the abuser will change.

These concepts can, admittedly, be hard to recognize. As parents, we often see what we want to see in our teens and their friends, rather than recognizing what is right in front of us. Here are some specific questions to help you determine whether your teen's dating relationship is healthy or unhealthy:

- As a couple, do they isolate themselves a majority of the time?

- As a couple, do they seem comfortable showing physical affection in public?

- Has either one of them changed their appearance or behavior to please the other person?

- When they spend time with their family and friends without the other person present, do they act sad, angry, frustrated, or inconvenienced?

- Do they tell each other that they love each other?

- Do they get extremely defensive when someone expresses concern about the seriousness of the relationship or their dependency on one another?

- Are you hearing rumors about their relationship?

If you answered yes to a majority of these questions, there might be reason for concern. It doesn't mean that sexual activity has already taken place, but it often means that the teen's relationship is progressing to deeper levels of attachment.

IS A BREAKUP POSSIBLE, IMMINENT—OR NECESSARY?

If you feel like your teen is demonstrating concerning changes that seem to stem from an unhealthy dating relationship, often the best outcome is for the teens to break up.

The good news is that almost all teen relationships end, and most don't last very long. Whether they know it or not, your teen is not yet mature enough to have a true long-term relationship. The bad news is that the process of ending something that's already begun is harder than building boundaries and preventing dangerous situations in the first place.

Ideally, your teen will **self-discover** that their relationship is unhealthy or detrimental and will end it without your interference. More often, though, a teen needs assistance to prompt the self-discovery process.

If you find yourself in this type of predicament, be as available as you can for your teen, and talk to them as much as possible, on as many different topics as possible. Your teen needs to know that you support them and will not reject them.

When it's appropriate within the context of your conversation, ask one or two leading questions:

- Are you pretending everything is okay?

- Do you have a nagging feeling about him/her that you keep ignoring?

- Are people you trust sharing their concerns?

- Do you ever feel limited, smothered, or lonely in the relationship?

- Is dating this person stifling your ability to develop your own personal strengths and abilities?

- Since you've been dating this person, has your overall outlook for the future changed?

- Are you continuing to endure unpleasant situations with this individual?

- Are you constantly feeling pressured by this individual—to do what they want to do, go where they want to go, look the way they want you to look, etc.?

- Do you cry a lot?

- Does it make you mad when other people talk about your relationship?

- Do you ever question why you are still dating this person?

- Does the person believe different things than you do?

- Are you dating for the sake of dating?

- Are you aware that this relationship doesn't have much of a chance to last a lifetime?

It's important that as parents we don't ask our teen all of these questions at one time. Instead, look for opportunities to challenge their thinking during regular, everyday conversations. Listen to what they're telling you, and let your teen's observations and comments show you how and when to dig deeper into what's really bothering them.

If your teen answers yes to several of these questions, try not to squash their own self-discovery by jumping in with statements like "See, I told you this wasn't a good idea" or "It's obvious you don't like him/her anymore; why don't you just break up?" These types of statements can shut down the teen's processing pattern. And for some teens, your disapproval will push them to stay in the relationship for the sake of proving you wrong.

If you feel like your teen has made an astute observation, take a break, let a day or so pass, and then revisit the process with additional questions. Try to listen more than you talk, and gently prompt the teen to truly consider the comprehensive impact this relationship can have on their life.

Once your teen is ready to make major changes in their relationship, they will need your emotional assistance. Help them work through their own answers to these questions:

Are you ready to make changes? If your teen can verbally state to someone safe that it's time to move on, that's a great first step.

What is your plan for saying goodbye? Role-play "the breakup" with your teen and encourage them to end the relationship in person. Unless the relationship is somehow physically dangerous, this is not the place for text messages. Encourage your teen to meet the other person in a public location, like a coffee shop, and to keep the conversation short. They don't need to go into detail or get drawn into an argument about their decision.

How can I help you change your normal routine? Is there a new, healthy pastime you would like to try? Assist your teen in creating a plan of action for changing their daily routine to adjust to the lack of the person in their life. Identify a healthy substitute, timewise, to replace what was possibly becoming toxic.

Once you follow through, who will hold you accountable? Challenge your teen to identify solid, mature individuals in their lives who will be willing to hold them accountable to their breakup.

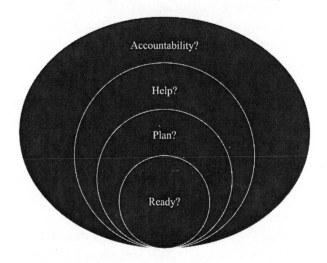

WHEN YOUR TEEN REFUSES TO BREAK UP

Humans have free will. Free will means that we can have our own opinions and make our own decisions. There may be a time when you can see that a relationship is unhealthy, but your teen adamantly refuses to let go.

This is a difficult situation. In my observation, most parents who try to force a breakup only end up alienating themselves from their teen, who may rebel against a mandate they disagree with.

A healthier goal is to take an incremental approach, focusing on implementing agreed-on consequences for any actual infractions of expectations or boundaries, while also investing time and energy into helping your teen to develop other aspects of their lives and broaden their thinking.

Teens in an unhealthy dating relationship often have tunnel vision and can only see their future as they've imagined it with their boyfriend or girlfriend. When a parent strategically places the teen in environments that challenge this limited perspective or eliminate the tunnel vision, often the teen begins to recognize the bigger picture and the reason for concern.

They also have relatively short attention spans, and as we've talked about, infatuation tends to fade quickly when it's not regularly fed with attention. So unless you are physically concerned for their safety, look for ways to redirect your teen.

Could they travel to visit their grandparents, friends, or out-of-state family members over a school holiday? Could they go on a retreat or mission trip with their church youth group? Is it time for your teen son or daughter to get a job and spend their time more productively? Is there a sport or extracurricular activity that your teen could try? If you have an adult friend or family member who your teen likes and trusts, could you enlist their help to come up with projects or activities? Sometimes a teen needs to feel like they're needed and have something to contribute, and that involvement will give them a broader perspective.

MY TEEN'S HEART IS BROKEN

I could hear her crying from down the hall. By the time I got to her bedroom my teen daughter's face was drenched in tears. Her boyfriend, out of the blue, had broken up with her. He'd shattered her heart, and now her dad and I were left to figure out how to help her make sense of it all. We held her; I cried with her, and then we helped her pick up the pieces.

Most of us have experienced at least one breakup in our lifetime.

Even if we were hoping that our son or daughter's relationship wouldn't last, being on the receiving end of a breakup absolutely stinks.

How do we help our teen through this? And how do we process our own feelings about this person who broke our daughter or son's heart?

Consider these tips to get your teen—and yourself—moving in the right direction:

1. **Be an amazing listener.** Right now, more than anything, your teen needs someone to just listen and allow them to process through their new status.

2. **Don't coulda woulda shoulda.** Now is not the time to say "I told you so" or "I knew this was going to happen." Help your teen get past their own questions about what they could have done differently, and encourage them not to beat themselves up. In time, as emotions fade, your teen may be ready to look at their own behavior and consider how to act in future situations, but first they need to grieve.

3. **No bashing allowed.** You may have had doubts about their boyfriend or girlfriend before the break-up, and now, as you watch your teen suffer, those thoughts might be amplified and brewing. On the other side, you may have really liked the other person and are personally feeling their loss from your family's lives. Whatever you think about them, don't say it. Hold your tongue. This is your teen's time to heal. Stick with, "I'm right here when you need me."

4. **Get creative.** Your teen needs to replace what used to be their norm with new, healthy, and creative distractions. Help them do so with intention and purpose. Use this time as an opportunity to spend time together as a family. Take day trips on the weekends, sign up for a class together, or take on a volunteer project as a family. Change things up and add some unique adventure to your experiences together.

5. **Hand your teen the scissors.** Partner with your son or daughter to cut the proverbial cord and take a break from communicating with their ex. Help them understand the importance of not chasing or begging for another conversation. Communicating in any format makes an already hard situation more difficult. There's a reason the breakup occurred. Help your teen trust that it's in their best interest to move on.

6. **Take a break.** Depending on how long your teen was in the relationship, it's probably a good idea for them to not jump into a new dating relationship for a while. Rushing in to a new relationship is definitely not the way to mend a broken heart. Help your teen understand that doing so will only add emotion to an already emotional situation.

Dating is a complex and charged enterprise. You and your teen will both probably make mistakes along the way. But keep at it, consider it a family collaborative effort and keep communicating.

11

HOW FAR IS TOO FAR?

T HE reality is that at some point your teen will have the opportunity to be alone with a person they're physically attracted to. As we explored earlier, your teen is a sexual being and craves physical touch. So instead of worrying if it will happen, the more important questions for us to ask are: When will it happen? Does your teen know how to handle the temptation? Do they know what their physical boundaries are? And are they comfortable expressing their physical boundaries?

At a time when "dating" often gets equated to "hooking up," our teens need help understanding how to counter the message that casual sexual contact is no big deal. Well before they start dating, they need to know how much physical affection is appropriate in a dating relationship, and what might end up hurting them or compromising their physical and emotional safety.

I often use the following set of questions in the classroom to help students explore "how far is too far." You could also use them to start a dialogue with your own teen.

1. *What represents the highest level of physical affection in a relationship?*

The obvious answer is sexual intercourse. (This is a good opportunity to remind them that sexual intercourse involves more than just penetration; as we'll explore later in the chapter, many teens today put oral sex in its own, less intimate category.)

2. *What shows the highest level of <u>commitment</u> in a relationship?*

It might take some conversation to help students get to the place where they see that marriage—legally binding, "'til death do us part" promises—is the pinnacle of commitment. They may point to the financial and practical commitments of living together or even argue for basic monogamy, regardless of legal status or lifestyle, as an equal form of commitment. This is an opportunity for you to reinforce the connection between long-term commitment and the healthy development of intimacy.

At this point, I explain that the only way for a relationship to be healthy is for it to be **balanced**. If the amount of physical affection in a relationship is greater than the amount of commitment, negative consequences are more likely.

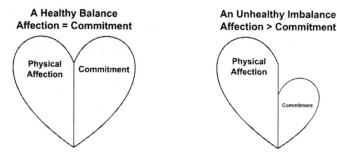

3. *What types of physical affection put you and your future at risk if the commitment of marriage is not in place?*

Any time body fluids come into contact with body openings, there's a risk. And any time there's skin-to-skin contact in the underwear zone, there's also a risk. Even casual contact can lead to STIs and their resulting diseases, and sexual intercourse can lead to an unplanned pregnancy.

THE NATURAL SEXUAL PROGRESSION

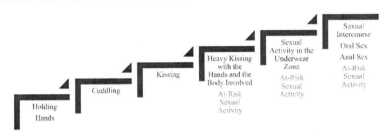

Most teens and young adults who are exploring their sexual desire for the first time follow a fairly similar, natural progression. Holding hands leads to cuddling, which leads to kissing, which leads to heavy kissing with hands and bodies involved, which leads to sexual activity in the "underwear zone," which eventually leads to sexual intercourse—the highest level of physical affection that one person can share with another person. Sequences similar to this are often described as the steps of physical affection, sexual foreplay, or the body's natural progression for sexual activity.

Each step of this progression can be exciting and satisfying on its own—at first. The first time your teen holds hands with someone they "like," it's going to be fun and exciting. But as they continue to hold hands, it becomes a normal part of the relationship, which means they might not experience the same sensation. This is because the sexual urges in the body are ready to move forward to the next step. So the teen naturally desires the sensation and decides to start cuddling and kissing...and so on and so forth, all the way to intercourse.

As a person has more experience with a higher level of physical affection, it's hard to go backwards and find the same level of excitement and discovery. And different people respond to the progressions at different speeds. In general, teen boys are more quickly and easily sexually stimulated. But both boys and girls need to understand that their bodies are naturally curious and will push them forward, and so it's important to set boundaries ahead of time—and to have a plan in place to maintain the boundary.

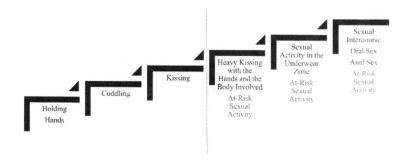

Challenge both your sons and daughters to set explicit goals for where they will "draw their line." Encourage them to remember that their bodies will naturally want to progress to the next form of physical intimacy, so thinking that they can safely move too high up the steps could be risky.

When you talk to your teen, it's important to stress that the sexual desire they are (or will be) experiencing is not wrong—it's natural, normal, and healthy. What is **unhealthy** is to allow that natural desire to control their choices, which could eventually change their future.

From a health perspective, setting a boundary beyond simple kissing can lead to unwanted consequences. It's easy to get carried away and end up with skin-to-skin contact in the underwear zone, which carries risks of infection and physical consequences, not to mention feelings of frustration and dissatisfaction as bodies push toward the next, more intimate level. That frustration often leads to intense relational stress, usually ending with arguments or feelings of shame or guilt.

Many teens want to experiment and engage in sexual activity so desperately they play around with the idea of "technical virginity" or what many kids call "everything but [sex]." This allows a teen to say they're a virgin because they've stopped before vaginal penetration by the penis. Teens have different reasons for this: they may want to avoid pregnancy or avoid the guilt or emotional consequences of "having sex." However, technical virginity still has a long list of possible consequences. Any teen who is experimenting with skin-to-skin contact in the underwear zone, or body fluids and body openings, is at risk for STIs.

ORAL SEX

Warning: we're going to get a little graphic here. I know this may not be a subject you want to think about for two or three pages, but I assure you, your teen has heard plenty about oral sex already, and there are things you need to know.

For over a decade, the media has been full of stories about how middle and high school students are engaging in oral sex at an alarming rate. According to the reports, it's something that girls do for boys, but not the other way around. For years, rumors of "rainbow parties," where middle school girls at a party would each wear a different shade of lipstick and perform oral sex on all the boys, leaving each with a "rainbow" of colors at the end, filled talk shows and magazine pages.

While some of that may just be media hype,[56] it's clear that kids today certainly know what oral sex is. Hollywood has not shied away from showing oral sex in increasing detail and usually not in the context of a committed relationship, let alone a marriage. When I ask students directly in the classroom about oral sex, while discussing at-risk sexual activity, one class will tell me it happens all the time on school buses, on school campuses, at teen parties, and at home, right under the parents' noses, and the next class will be totally grossed out by the topic and act like it never happens.

During these conversations, some teens share that in their opinion, oral sex is a casual event of no great importance, meaning it's not sexual intercourse. What teens often don't realize is that oral sex is, legally and medically, a form of sexual intercourse, which comes with a long list of possible consequences. A person can get an STI through oral sex. Syphilis, herpes, and gonorrhea throat infections are transmitted through oral sex. To a lesser degree, chlamydia and human papillomavirus are also transmittable via oral sex, and even HIV is occasionally transmitted by oral sex.[57]

With the stakes being so high related to possible infection or disease transmission, as parents, we have to set aside our discomfort and discuss the risks. Once again, body fluids are coming into contact with body openings, not to mention the social components often related to oral sex.

Here are some suggestions to help you through the conversation:

- Share with your teen that oral sex is actually a form of sexual intercourse and not an option to preserve their "technical virginity."

- Discuss the physical risks involved in oral sex and how body fluids being in contact with body openings can transmit infection.[58] Your teen may not agree with you about the emotional or social significance of the issue, especially if their peers are giving them a different message, but the science of potential health risks can't be debated.

- Equip your teen with a practical response if the subject comes up. For example: "Oral sex can cause cancer in my mouth, so I'm not interested."

- Use this as an opportunity to talk about their community of friends and the types of peer pressure they face. Challenge your teen to consider if the people they're hanging out with are pressuring unhealthy behavior. If the answer to this question is "yes," your teen might need some assistance reevaluating their relationships.

Having this delicate and definitely uncomfortable conversation with your teen allows you to once again address boundaries, but more importantly, it's an opportunity to talk about your teen's feelings of self-worth. Discussions like this often prompt additional conversations and possibly challenge the teen to consider what they hope their future spouse, assuming they marry someday, is saving for them. Encourage them to start respecting their future relationship today, even if it's still an incomprehensibly long time away.

SEXUAL PROGRESSION IN A "HOOKING UP" CULTURE

The traditional sexual progression I describe earlier is how most teens, and individuals in general, progress intimately.

But times have changed, and the "friends with benefits" and "hooking up" culture sees sexual progression in a totally different way. A lot of physical intimacy takes place outside the context of a relationship.

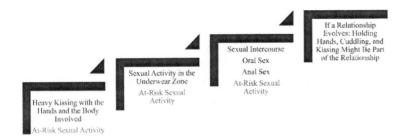

Heavy Kissing with the Hands and the Body Involved
At-Risk Sexual Activity

Sexual Activity in the Underwear Zone
At-Risk Sexual Activity

Sexual Intercourse
Oral Sex
Anal Sex
At-Risk Sexual Activity

If a Relationship Evolves: Holding Hands, Cuddling, and Kissing Might Be Part of the Relationship

Within many teen communities, there is an attitude that getting together in an unchaperoned, no-strings-attached setting for the purpose of "hooking up" with someone, or with more than one person, is okay. It's hard to imagine, but it happens. And it definitely comes with consequences. I've met too many teen girls who are trying to make sense of the emotional and physical baggage that they are struggling through due to this type of lifestyle choice.

My heart hurts for these girls who are gambling with their hearts and bodies, hoping for as little long-term damage as possible. If only they understood that sex is not a game, not frivolous, not a consequence-free pastime. Sex is *always* life-changing and can be life-threatening. Teens are consistently being led to believe that sleeping with countless no-strings-attached partners is a paradise, but in between the seductive games and sexual triumphs, they are actually enslaving themselves to a sexual lifestyle that doesn't fulfill their desires.

To tackle this, communication and boundary setting is, again, the key. As your teen son or daughter approaches their dating season of life, keep the channels of communication open and ask specific, guiding questions like:

- What boundaries have you set?
- How will you communicate your boundaries to your date?
- Will the individual you are dating respect your boundaries?
- Within this boundary, what kinds of behaviors are safe?
- Within this boundary, what behaviors are definitely out-of-bounds?
- Are there particular peers, environments, or behaviors that tend to pressure you to compromise the boundary you have set?

Parents, have hope! Some of you might be feeling overwhelmed right about now. Although there is plenty to be concerned about surrounding the teen dating scene, there is also hope. Your teen needs your support. While you cannot wave a magic wand and make your daughter or son do exactly what you would like, you can encourage them, educate them, and empower them to set high standards for the dating season of life.

PART 5: WHAT IF?

My name is Samantha. I am seventeen years old, and I am the mother of a beautiful baby girl.

When I turned sixteen, I was the star volleyball hitter for my high school team, and my boyfriend was the star defensive end for the football team. One Friday night in October, I had an away volleyball game, and he had an away football game, and we both got back to the school around 12:30 a.m. The buses left, and everyone jumped in their cars and headed home.

But we got in his car and started making out, which eventually led to going too far. I knew it was not okay, but I kept telling myself it was okay. We had never said "I love you" to each other before, but that night, we did. I went home feeling really strange, totally different than I thought I would after my first time having sex. I felt really guilty and really happy at the same time. I really can't explain it.

About six weeks later, I was feeling weird, and we figured out I was pregnant. I did everything I could to ignore the fact. I cried a lot, and I was really mean to my boyfriend. If it weren't for the ladies at the medical pregnancy center, we would not have gotten through the initial panic. Thankfully, my boyfriend was a really good guy. He told me that he would always be there for me and that we would get through this.

It was time to tell our families. Both families were shocked, disappointed, and angry, but eventually, they calmed down and started to help us plan how we were going to co-parent the child. We met with a counselor several times and worked through the hard details related to a teen pregnancy, finishing school and co-parenting. *Eight months later, we had a beautiful baby girl with red curly hair and big green eyes just like me, her mommy. We named her Alexa.*

Alexa is now one, and her father and I are seniors in high school. To be honest, I don't know if we are still boyfriend and girlfriend. Now we are kind of Mom and Dad. Our parents share the time taking care of Alexa while we are at school, and I take a few of my classes online. I am no longer playing volleyball, which is really hard, but we did agree that it would be good for the father of the baby to continue his football career. We are both planning on going to college. It will definitely be different than we had originally planned, and it will take me longer than it will take my boyfriend, but I am willing to accept that. Everything we do at this point is based on how can we make the best out of this difficult situation and what is best for Alexa.

Yes, it's been really hard. And we are not sure exactly what the future holds. We are kind of taking this one day at a time. Sometimes when Alexa calls me Mommy and reaches to give me a hug, I get this strange feeling in my stomach. I still can't believe I'm a mom. It's odd and awesome all wrapped into one sweet little smiling girl. As hard as this is, I'm glad she's in my life, and I'm really thankful for the support system that we have. It would be really hard to do this without both of our families.

12

WHAT IF MY TEEN IS HAVING SEX?

Most parents don't think it will happen to them. They hope it doesn't happen to them. But then they walk into a room, or read a text, or get a phone call from another parent, and suddenly it feels like everything changes.

What should you do if you find out that your teen is sexually active? How we choose to handle the situation will impact how our teen reacts and the eventual outcome. Here are some suggestions to help you get started. Consider these in light of your own family and needs.

Try to respond, instead of react. It's normal to be disappointed or even to feel betrayed if your son or daughter has been lying to you, but focusing on the disappointment will not solve the issue.

Give yourself some time to process the news after you find out, and set a specific time to sit down and talk through the situation with your teen. Think about what you want to say and how you will present your concerns to your teen. They will probably not be happy about the discussion, and their embarrassment at getting "caught" may lead them to be aggressive or withdrawn. Don't allow that to stop you. Focus on your teen's future and how the choice to be sexually active could greatly hinder it.

Ask open-ended questions, and listen to what your teen says. An open-ended or neutral question, such as "Where do you see your relationship going?" will help your teen not shut down. Judgmental questions like "How could you have done this?" often drive a deeper wedge between you and may push them toward their peers and their relationship for support.

Do everything you can to help your teen connect their current choices with the future by using specific and conclusive open-ended questions. For example:

- How are you going to financially support a child if you get/she gets pregnant?

- What is the plan for your relationship once high school is over?

- How has your choice to be sexually active changed your relationship?

- How has your choice to be sexually active changed your reputation and your relationship with your friends?

- How do you feel this relationship is helping you develop yourself as an individual?

You can't force them into self-discovery, and you may not like the answers you hear. In the end, you are still the parent, and they're still children, and it's your responsibility to set guidelines and consequences for their behavior, even if they're "in love" and have a plan for the future. But in every stage of this journey, try to honor your son or daughter as individuals with free will and engage them in the decisions that need to be made.

Listen more than you talk. Don't interrupt their responses. And be careful with your own body language. This is an area I personally struggle with in parenting, because everything I'm feeling comes across in my expression and the way I hold myself. But I know that crossing my arms, rolling my eyes, and pointing fingers are all types of nonverbal reactions that diminish a reasonable conversation.

Talk about the big picture. Instead of getting caught up in the details of a single situation or event where your teen got "caught," focus the conversation on the larger goals of long-term good health and meaningful relationships. Be prepared to explain how teen sexual activity can diminish opportunities for college, independence, travel, and other dreams.

Don't assume that just because your teen chose to be sexually active that they've thought through the consequences.

Evaluate whether this is an appropriate time for discipline. Presumably, your teen's decision to engage in sexual activity involved breaking some specific guidelines that you set in advance. At the very least, they have betrayed your trust. Recognize and clearly communicate what the disciplinary consequences are for their behavior, and then be prepared to follow through. If you haven't predetermined consequences, then take the time to consider your options and engage with your spouse, if appropriate, to make sure you're on the same page. If you impulsively ground your teen from using the phone or car for a period of time, be prepared for the inconvenience and extra effort that will cost you. If you tell your teen that they're not allowed to socialize with their friends for a month, does that include homecoming? Is it prom season? Is a spring break trip already planned? Consistency is key here. Unenforced discipline sends a dangerous message that leads a teen to create a false sense of entitlement, freedom, and control.

No matter what, don't tear them down. This is a sensitive time, and it's hard to not condemn your teen. But it's also hard to condemn your teen's actions without appearing to condemn them as a person. Your teen is experiencing all kinds of emotions already about their sexual activity and now feel the shame of having to face it in front of their parents. It's important to protect their self-worth. If in the heat of the conversation, you tear down your teen as a person—their intelligence, their morals, their ability to make decisions—or if you mock their feelings, you may push them away from you and toward those who make them feel like they have value—even if it's false value.

Try not to say things like "I am so ashamed of you" or ask "How could you do this to us?" It's natural to feel these types of emotions. Your teen has betrayed you on some level. But more than that, they're betraying themselves. Instead of pouring your emotions all over the situation, extend grace and put an action plan in place for moving forward.

THE BIRTH CONTROL QUESTION

Many parents, when faced with the knowledge that their teen has become—or may become—sexually active, make an appointment with the family doctor to get a birth control prescription for their daughter or leave a box of condoms conspicuously on their son's bedside table. Even if they believe that their teen is too young to be sexually active, they respond to their own fears of pregnancy and justify it as being "proactive."

"We can't stop them," more than one parent has told me. "At least we can protect them." There are a number of logical problems with this approach, though. For one, it sends an incredibly confusing message to our teens. Are parents telling them to not have sex or not?

Do parents buy cigarettes for their teens if they find out they've smoked a few cigarettes with their friends? What if a child wants to cut school—would a parent call the school and withdraw them? Of course not. So why do so many parents give up when it comes to their teen's involvement in sexual activity?

Facilitating teen sex is just as dangerous as ignoring it.

Providing birth control as an easy solution to an uncomfortable problem might seem "responsible," but the realities of this problem are more complex than stopping at the drug store. Earlier in the book, we discussed the difference between eliminating the physical, social, financial, and psychological consequences of teen sexual activity and only reducing the physical risks of teen sexual activity. It's the difference between "safe" sex and "safer" sex.

A teen who has chosen to be sexually active can make a decision to stop engaging in at-risk sexual activity. It really comes down to the parent-teen relationship, the education provided, and the way in which the situation is handled. Where you are today doesn't have to determine where you are tomorrow.

EMERGENCY CONTRACEPTION

At the women's clinic, we get phone calls and texts almost every day from girls—and parents—with questions about emergency contraception (EC), which is more commonly known as the "morning-after pill." Like most aspects of sexual activity, there are no easy answers. EC has brought questions, debates, disagreements, controversy, and solutions to what was already a very complex conversation.

EC is intended to prevent pregnancy after known or suspected contraceptive failure, unprotected intercourse, or forced sex. These pills, sold over-the-counter (within seventy two hours of sex) or by prescription (within five days of sex), are marketed as the magical solution to a mistake and a way to eliminate the risks of pregnancy after the decision to have sex is already made.

Unfortunately, it's not quite that simple and clear.

The science behind EC is similar to birth control pills. Some are single-pill doses that contain a large amount of the same progestin hormone found in common birth control pills; they work primarily by preventing the egg and the sperm from meeting. Others are progesterone-blocking hormones that may reduce the chance of pregnancy by preventing or postponing ovulation. It is also possible that an emergency contraceptive pill could prevent (or disrupt) a fertilized egg or embryo from implanting in the uterus and continuing to develop.[59]

The use of emergency contraception is a topic that all families need to research and discuss within the home. Here are a few key points to ponder:

- Do you believe that fertilization (rather than the implantation of the fertilized egg) is the starting point of human life?

- Would using emergency contraception result in an embryo's death?

In addition to the difficult and controversial questions listed above, it's important for families to be aware of the potential physical side effects for teens selecting to use EC, including:

- Nausea

- Vomiting

- Change in menstrual periods

- Lower abdominal pain

- Fatigue

- Headaches

- Dizziness

- Breast tenderness

- Menstrual cramps[60]

There is no risk-free way to undo a sexual decision once it's been made.

CREATING A PLAN FOR A NEW BEGINNING

Once you find out that your teen is sexually active, your challenge becomes helping that teen step back from their behavior and begin again. As we saw in the last chapter, that's not an easy endeavor. The body tends to progress forward sexually, and it's hard to stop doing what it's already accustomed to.

To start over, both you and your teen need a plan.

The hardest part of looking at new beginnings is understanding what to do with the existing teen relationship. In almost every situation, the best thing is for the couple to break up so that they can each establish their new boundaries and beginnings without the pressure of the other. However, if it's at all possible, the breakup should come from the teens themselves and not be imposed by the parents.

If Romeo and Juliet taught us anything, it's that forbidden love is twice as appealing. Telling your daughter or son that they *can't* be with someone anymore might invite increased rebellion, and I only recommend doing it as a last resort.

As parents, you can use the strategies shared throughout this book to help lead your teen to their own conclusions about the health of the relationship, and you can use consequences of their behavior to limit the couple's time together. Taken with the emotional stress already on the relationship, based on the entanglement of sexual activity, most teen relationships naturally fade and go their separate ways.

Additionally, here are a few ideas to help you start thinking about what will be best for your family moving forward.

Can you:

- Proactively **change** their schedule/routine, surroundings, and the people who influence them? Maybe it's time for your teen to get a job and start acting more responsible. In extreme cases, they may need to change schools or spend time during school breaks visiting an out-of-town friend or relative.

- Help your teen **predetermine what their new physical boundary will be** in reference to future relationships? Encourage your teen to practice verbally stating their boundary.

- Strongly suggest that your teen **not date for a while**? Jumping into a new relationship will not solve the problem. It will add fuel to an already burning fire.

- Help your teen **evaluate the tempting environments that led to their behavior**? If the sexual activity took place at a friend's house where supervision is lax or alone in a car or in a place that only your teen has access to, put a plan of action in place to identify and eliminate these environments.

- Identify a solid person or a counselor who will lovingly **hold the teen accountable** and check in with the teen on a regular basis? Sometimes teens, who are processing through their uniqueness and separateness from their families, are more willing to share with a different, trusted adult. Does your teen have a coach, mentor, youth leader, pastor, aunt or uncle, or other adult friend who can listen to things they may not want to share with Mom and Dad?

If your teen has been engaging in risky sexual activity, including any skin-to-skin contact in the underwear zone or body fluids touching body openings, they need to schedule a doctor's appointment to be tested for STIs. Many teens, at this stage, will also benefit from professional counseling to help them process through what led them to their behavior and how to change. Sexual activity is typically a symptom of deeper issues like insecurity, a need for approval, boredom, peer pressure, curiosity, etc.

Before you go, make sure that your doctor and counselor are aware of your perspective on birth control and teen sexual activity. Many doctors will automatically advise birth control if they meet with a sexually active teen, which might send a confusing or contradictory message. If this happens, be prepared to explain the facts right away: that no birth control can protect their thoughts, feelings, or future, nor can it provide 100% physical protection.

IF YOUR TEEN WON'T STOP ENGAGING IN AT-RISK SEXUAL ACTIVITY

Like it or not, our children have free will, and the messages coming at them about sex are strong. It's heartbreaking to even think about this, but some children will rebel. They'll refuse to change their sexual behavior even after they get caught. They will suffer the consequences, and push back, and make decisions over and over that put their future body and heart at risk.

I can't tell you what you, as parents, should do about this. There are no perfect answers. I know families who have, after months of anguish, agreed to a birth control plan for their teen daughter, even at the expense of their principles. I know other families who have disowned their rebellious teens, cutting them off both emotionally and financially, even in high school, until the son or daughter "repented." And I've heard hundreds of stories that fall somewhere in between.

If your son or daughter refuses to consider changing their sexual behavior, you and your spouse, if appropriate, need to evaluate what's truly in your teen and your family's best interest. Be honest and realistic about the situation.

If your teen is living in rebellion and making unhealthy sexual choices, don't ignore it. If possible, bring together your teen, his or her boyfriend or girlfriend, and, if possible, the parents of the other teen. Ask hard questions like:

- If there are consequences to their behavior, are they prepared to take financial and practical responsibility for the consequences?

- If pregnancy happens, what will they do?

- When high school ends, what is their plan with regard to the relationship?

- How is their decision impacting younger siblings?

Your teen is making adult choices; they need to be part of the adult decision process. If they don't know the answers at first or try to blow off your questions, give them a time frame to come up with a plan, and then follow up. Keep following up.

This is part of what being an adult is, and your teen is choosing adult behavior.

Most importantly of all, don't give up and keep loving them.

13

WHAT IF MY TEEN IS PREGNANT?

As we've seen, in the heat of sexual passion, teens rarely think about the ramifications of their decision to engage in sexual activity. Or at least they don't until a girl's period is late. Who should she tell? What should she do?

According to the Guttmacher Institute, nearly 615,000 girls between fifteen and nineteen years old become pregnant each year.[61] For most teens, it's a difficult and life-defining moment, full of fear, confusion, guilt, and often denial. Teens are often tempted to keep a pregnancy secret for as long as possible, thinking that if they ignore the situation, it will just go away. Too many teens assume that their parents will be angry and unreasonable, and they choose to just "take care of" the situation themselves.

The moment when your daughter or son tells you about a pregnancy is probably the hardest you will ever face as a parent. Any mix of emotions and thoughts can race through your mind: surprise, shock, denial, anger, grief, loss, compassion, alternatives, perhaps even joy—all of which are considered normal and understandable. The repercussions—for your child; for *their* child; for you, the parent, and maybe even the rest of the family—are staggering.

I've seen families in this situation rise up, work together, and create a positive outcome in the midst of a difficult time. I've also seen the opposite, where families carry bitterness into arguments that seem to last for the entire pregnancy and then continue to carry the pain with them for years to come.

We cannot change the past, but we can choose how we respond in the present—even in the face of overwhelming feelings. How do we show love in the midst of our legitimate disappointment? Will we allow this situation to build into resentment, or will we take a deep breath and move toward the best-case scenario possible for the teen pregnancy? Choosing to do the latter is not easy, but it is the best way to protect our teen and our relationship with our teen.

If you find yourself facing this situation, here are some immediate suggestions, based on our counseling sessions with parents at the medical pregnancy center.

- **Remain calm with your teen.** This is easier said than done, but the way that you act in the first few minutes or days will set the stage for your home for months to come.

- **Graciously comfort your teen.** When you want to say, "I told you this would happen!" say instead, "We will get through this." Positive self-talk is known to impact how we handle crises.

- **Take a time out.** If you need an outlet for your emotions, excuse yourself to a private place. Retreat into your bedroom, meet a trusted friend for lunch, go see a movie by yourself, get a massage, take a walk outside, etc. Regroup, gather your thoughts, and release your emotions.

- **Contact your local medical pregnancy center.** They will provide an immediate support system that extends compassion to you and your teen in the midst of this situation. If you're not sure where to find a center, you can find a directory at http://www.optionline.org/ and http://pregnancydecisionline.org/.

- **Allow the experts to care for your daughter.** If you choose to go to a medical pregnancy center, understand that the trained professionals have a plan for lovingly caring for your daughter during this time of confusion and anxiety. The appointment might not go as quickly as you would like. The conversation might make you

feel uncomfortable. But allow the care team to work through pregnancy verification, a decision guide, the ultrasound, and options
education with your daughter.

- **Get educated.** Education about fetal development, the father of
the baby's role, your daughter's health, and her options will help
you and your teen process through the situation and determine
what is best for everyone involved.

THREE OPTIONS

When a teenage girl comes to our medical pregnancy center, whether
with her parents, the father of the baby, or alone, she's usually nervous,
emotional, and overwhelmed. She's also full of questions. Our nurses
often hear some variations of questions like:

> *My friends are telling me to take the morning-after pill. Will it
> work? Is it safe?*
>
> *Is there a simple solution to my problem? Can I make this go away
> so that my parents never find out?*
>
> *What can I do about the people who are pressuring me?*
>
> *Can I have a baby and still live my life?*
>
> *If I place my child for adoption, will I ever see the baby?*
>
> *Can I still go to college?*

Facing an unplanned pregnancy is hard. Both the teen mother and
the father typically must process through questions, fear, confusion, and
anger. There are critical, life-changing choices to be made. Whatever
they decide, pregnancy has made them parents. Some are eager for the
role; some are not. But these new parents are able to legally decide the
future of a new life, and education is the key to making the best decision
possible.

When it comes to pregnancy, teenagers basically have three choices:

1. Parent the child

2. Place the child for adoption

3. Abort the child

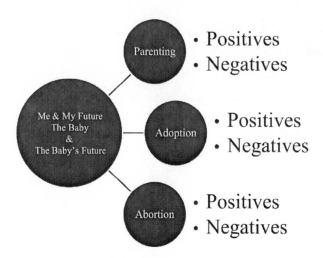

Each one, like the significant life decisions that the teens made that brought them to this place, have physical, psychological, social, and financial impacts that they'll need to consider. Let's look at each one.

OPTION #1: PARENTING THE CHILD

- **Physically:** This option involves pregnancy to full term and child-birth, both of which have possible risks and complications for a female body.

- **Psychologically:** The teen parent will have memories of her life and hopes from before the pregnancy. They will face fears, confusion, and the stress of adult responsibilities. But they will also experience the honor of being a parent, joy from creating a new life, and an emotional connection to the baby they chose to have.

- **Socially:** The teen mother, and possibly both parents, will probably experience restricted freedom during and after the pregnancy as they adjust to physical changes and adult responsibilities. Many of their teen friends will have a hard time relating to someone who can't hang out because they have a baby. Other adults and mentors will step up and support them in their decision to parent the child.

- **Financially:** The average cost of raising a baby to their eighteenth birthday is almost $250,000.[62] Young parents also need to consider the potential costs of changing college plans and potential employment.

When a teen girl is trying to decide whether to keep and raise her child, she needs to consider all of her parenting options, which include:

- **Married parenting:** If the teen parents decide to get married, they should build a solid foundation by seeking premarital help from trusted parents, friends, church support groups, and professional counselors. A marriage can last a lifetime, even if the start seems a little rough.

- **Co-parenting:** Some teen parents choose to both be involved in their child's life but recognize that they aren't meant to be together as a couple. Mothers and fathers who enter into their parenting roles with a clear understanding that they will share responsibilities have a greater chance for success for the mother and the father and, inevitably, their child.

- **Single parenting:** If one parent chooses not to be involved, the other can still make a world of difference in a child's life. It's challenging to raise a child alone, but with the support of a community, it's possible.

- **Short-term care assistance:** Most states offer temporary foster care with loving families who can give a young mom a chance to get on her feet if she is unable to immediately raise and care for her child. In most of these situations, the teen parent can create a legal agreement that states the goal of resuming her parental role when she is able. If for some reason the plan fails, an adoption plan can still be implemented.

Choosing to become a teen parent is challenging, but with the support of friends, families, and community resources, it's a respectful, viable option that can bring joyful, positive results. The outcome of this option selection greatly depends on how the teen responds to the situation. If you and your teen are considering this choice, you need to think about not only what is in the teen's best interest but also what is in the best interest of the unborn child. Parenting is a huge, lifelong, and often thankless responsibility—you know that more than anyone, but your teen may not.

We meet a lot of girls who consider parenting their child because "babies are cute" or because they think that a child will love them unconditionally. (That's often the need that pushed them to sexual activity and pregnancy in the first place.) Your daughter—or son—needs to be prepared to take on this responsibility, even when it's difficult or inconvenient. They need to be ready to parent with courage and perseverance. In doing so, parenting often enriches the families' lives.

You can help them through this in a myriad of ways, depending on your relationship and what you are emotionally and practically capable of providing. Teen parents benefit in the long term by creating an education plan and finishing their degrees, but they often need child care and a solid support system to help them through school.

Most local medical pregnancy centers will provide families with a list of community resources for young, single parents, and many also offer long-term emotional support.

OPTION #2: PLACING THE CHILD FOR ADOPTION

- **Physically:** This option involves pregnancy to full term and childbirth, both of which have possible risks and complications for a female body.

- **Psychologically:** This often depends on the terms of the adoption and the perspective of the teen parents. The teen mom, especially, may struggle with memories of the birth and the baby. Both parents may feel sadness and grief from letting the child go, joy from creating a new life, and relief at doing what will give both them and the baby a strong future.

- **Socially:** The teen mom will experience some restricted freedom during the pregnancy. Her group of friends may support her or judge her based on her decisions to have sex in the first place and then to place the child for adoption.

- **Financially:** Some teen parents are responsible for finding ways to meet the initial medical costs of the pregnancy, though adoption placement agencies usually have resources to assist with this.

Adoption provides an opportunity for stable couples who want to raise families to be paired with children who need safe, supportive homes. In a recent national survey of adoptive families, 92% report that their adopted children have positive feelings about their adoptions.[63] Not only is adoption a caring choice for the unborn child, it offers the teen parents the opportunity to meet their own personal goals. Teens who aren't yet ready for the responsibility of raising a child can continue to mature and pursue their education or career in ways that are appropriate for their ages.

It takes considerable maturity, support, and selfless courage for teen parents to release a baby for adoption. Your medical pregnancy center can refer you to reputable adoption agencies in your area that can help your teens select the type of adoption—open, partially open, or confidential—and to generally assist the teen in the selection process and with actually releasing the child. Adoption placement agencies strive to meet the birth parents' desires related to the selected plan, release, and future contact with the child, and often they also provide professional counseling throughout the placement process. Doing so can help the teen reach a measure of emotional healing throughout the process and after the birth of the child.

Here are additional resources to help you dig deeper if you believe this is an area you need assistance with:

- http://adoption-share.com/

- http://www.impregnant.org/

- http://ichooseadoption.org/

- http://www.childwelfare.gov

OPTION #3: ABORTING THE CHILD

- **Physically:** Regardless of the type of abortion (medical or surgical), pregnancy termination carries some short-term and long-term medical risks, outlined below, including possible risks to a woman's future reproductive health.

- **Psychologically:** Teen parents who choose to abort typically express an initial feeling of relief, but carry a longer-term risk of post-abortion symptoms, a form of post-traumatic stress disorder (PTSD), which some women struggle with after an abortion. The teen mom, the father of the baby, and the parents of the teens may struggle with emotions of guilt, loss, depression, and grief.

- **Socially:** The teen mom may experience rejection or acceptance from peers and others, depending on their views of teen sexual activity and of abortion. If she chooses or is forced to keep the experience a secret, the emotional weight may cause additional side effects like social withdraw.

- **Financially:** The cost of the abortion procedure varies by location and is dependent upon how many weeks a woman is into her pregnancy and what procedure is being done. Also, there may be additional costs if long-term counseling is needed or if there are any medical complications from the abortion.

A quarter of teen pregnancies (177,250) each year end in induced abortions.[64] For many teens—and often their parents—there is a temptation to just "deal" with the "problem" quickly by selecting to abort. However, there are many things to consider before a decision is made:

- What types of procedures are available?

- What are the physical and immediate risks following an abortion?

- What cost is involved?

- What are the long-term physical risks?

- What are the long-term emotional risks?

- What are the long-term relational risks?

- What if I change my mind?

- What are the alternatives?

There are currently four different types of medical abortions and three different types of surgical abortions available. Which type of abortion can be performed is based on how far along a woman is in her pregnancy, based on the date of her last menstrual period (LMP). If she is unsure of the date of her LMP, a limited ultrasound can be performed.

Because of the highly politicized and emotional nature of this decision, it's difficult to get complete, unbiased information about the risks associated with induced abortions. Medical research indicates varying side effects and complications, including abdominal pain, severe cramping, nausea, vomiting, diarrhea, headaches, dizziness, heavy bleeding, infection, incomplete abortion, organ damage, and death.[65]

In addition to the risks already listed, teens who think they might want to have a baby later in life should be aware of the possible risks that an abortion might pose to future pregnancies, including placenta previa and premature births.[66]

ABORTION AND BREAST CANCER

For years there have been questions about a possible link between induced abortion and breast cancer. The concern is that an induced abortion interrupts the normal cycle of hormones in a woman's body during pregnancy. Some research shows that this interruption might increase a women's risk of developing breast cancer later in life.[67] Some research shows there is no link.[68] As the medical experts continue to debate the nature of the association, we're left with questions and risk,

Here are the facts that we know:

- When a woman becomes pregnant, her body begins to go through biological changes in order to prepare for childbirth. Increased levels of estrogen during pregnancy cause a woman's breasts to enlarge with cells that will eventually allow for milk production. By the time of a full-term birth these cells have differentiated into milk-producing tissue and have stopped multiplying, two factors that make them more resistant to cancer.[69]

- Carrying a pregnancy to full term, especially a first pregnancy be-fore the age of thirty, gives a measure of protection against breast cancer.[70]

- Several worldwide epidemiological studies of disease have repor-ted a positive association between a later development of breast cancer and induced abortion.[71]

- Miscarriages, unlike induced abortion, don't raise the risk of breast cancer because these pregnancies don't produce enough estrogen, which is the driving factor behind the growth of undifferentiated, cancer-vulnerable cells.[72]

THE PSYCHOLOGICAL SIDE OF ABORTION

Beyond the physical risks of abortion, there are psychological issues that may take years to work through. Many teens who have come through the medical clinic first report feeling "normal" and relieved that their crisis is over. However, many, though not all, post-abortive individuals share that they experienced significant emotional, relational, and spiritual issues months, or even years, later. Overall, abortion is more associated with more negative psychological outcomes when compared to miscarriage or carrying an unintended pregnancy to term.[73]

Teens, especially, are at risk. Compared to women who have induced abortions in adulthood, teens who abort:

- Are more likely to commit suicide.

- Are more likely to develop psychological problems.

- Are more likely to have troubled relationships.

- Are generally in need of more counseling and guidance regarding abortion.

- Are nearly three times more likely to be admitted to mental health hospitals than women in general.[74]

As we mentioned earlier, post-abortion symptoms often include emotional and physical symptoms similar to other forms of PTSD.[75] Post-abortive women often experience a consistent struggle to turn off feelings connected to the abortion and a vague feeling of emptiness and loss that lasts for years. Many experience a physical response when abortion is mentioned, such as tightening of their stomach muscles, clenching their jaw, breaking out into a sweat, or holding their breath.[76]

Abortion is a serious thing and not something to rush into in order to cover up or hide an unplanned "problem." Before a teen or family makes a decision about abortion, it's important that they visit a medical pregnancy center and talk to a trained nurse about their options. By getting pregnancy verification and a free ultrasound, the teen is truly informed and can make a decision based on information beyond the immediate crisis at hand.

Many teens believe choosing an abortion will preserve their relationship and will allow things to go back to the way they were before the pregnancy happened. Often, just the opposite is the case: abortion actually increases the risk for relationship failure and future relationship problems.[77]

For some individuals, abortion is an easy fix to a difficult situation. For others, it's not a successful solution, and new problems seem to arise. One seventeen-year-old girl, Holly, came to our clinic recently and shared this description of her experience:

> *I seriously regret my abortion. It caused me to be depressed and change as a person. I stopped hanging around my friends who tried to make me feel good or happy because I didn't think I deserved attention or love. I didn't tell my parents. They still don't know, but I'm pretty sure they are wondering why I'm so different. I have increased my alcohol intake significantly, hoping it will ease the pain and stop me from remembering what I did.*

In many states, a teenager is not legally required to get her parents' permission before she has an induced abortion, and so it's possible that you may find out after the fact that your daughter made a difficult decision on her own. If so, I highly recommend that you consult with a counselor trained in post-abortion recovery, either through a medical pregnancy center or in private practice. You and your daughter may both struggle with the long-term implications of her choice, and having someone to help you work through the unresolved psychological, physical, and spiritual reactions can help lead to closure and healing.

Here are additional resources to help you dig deeper if you believe this is an area you need assistance with:

- http://www.abortionrecovery.org/

- http://beforeyoudecide.info/

WHAT DOES YOUR DAUGHTER NEED?

When she discovers that she's pregnant as a teenager, your daughter is probably at the most vulnerable point of her entire life. Most teens facing an unplanned pregnancy experience so many destructive emotions and negative pressures that the *situation* may prove a greater threat to their well-being than the pregnancy itself. A *crisis pregnancy* often leads to the teen mom perceiving that the *people* or *circumstances* in her life are so threatening that her only way to cope is to shut down.

The greatest feeling is fear, which manifests in multiple forms. Fear of losing something or someone important. Fear of losing their plans for the future. Fear of losing her parents' approval. Whatever the fear, it's her fear, it's real, and it needs to be explored no matter how irrational, ridiculous, or selfish it may seem to you as her parents.

One of the best things you can do if your daughter becomes pregnant is to stay in communication with her. Work on reducing her immediate anxiety by letting her know that you are going to help her process through her choices—and then *be there* by:

- Listening as she talks about her feelings and pain.

- Acknowledging her feelings and pain, using self-growth statements like "I sense your disappointment" or "I know this is difficult."

- Encouraging rational, thoughtful decisions.

- Respecting her feelings about the baby's father.

- Understanding her need for time and privacy.

- Connecting her to counselors who share your values and are compassionate and educated in the field of unplanned pregnancies.

Your pregnant teen needs you now more than ever. However, it's important that in the process of supporting her you don't *enable* her. Don't make it too easy or make hard decisions for her. As difficult as it may be, she is in an adult situation and needs to begin thinking on an adult level. She needs to take responsibility for talking to the father of her child and his parents; to her school, friends, and others who may be affected; and to speak for herself during medical and counseling sessions.

WHAT DOES YOUR SON NEED?

As even the most basic of health classes will teach us, it takes two people to make a baby. So if your son comes to you with the news that his girlfriend is pregnant, you, too, are in for an emotional roller coaster.

Teen boys process pregnancy differently than teen girls, because it isn't something that is immediately affecting their bodies. Many of them are able to emotionally and physically distance themselves from the crisis, leaving the weight of the situation only on the girl. Others will naturally step up and take responsibility. Either way, once you get involved as his parents, it's important to understand his new position as a father.

If a pregnancy occurs, talk to your son and make sure that he understands his equal responsibility in the conception of a child. Talk to him about his new role as a father. Yes, you read that correctly—a baby has been created; therefore, *your son is already a father*! Challenge him to look at the big picture, while encouraging and supporting him as he processes through the forthcoming realities.

The laws concerning the rights of unwed fathers vary from state to state in the United States,[78] but there are a few realities that are constant across the board:

- A baby's father does *not* have a say in what option a pregnant mother chooses, nor even have input in her decision, *unless* the mother of the baby chooses to include him in the process.

- If the mother chooses to parent the child, the father—regardless of his age—will be financially responsible for his child until it turns eighteen years old. If he chooses not to pay child support, the mother of the baby can take him to court to have his wages garnished.

- If she chooses to place the child for adoption, the father typically has legal rights related to how he's notified and what input he can offer, which vary from state to state.

- By law, the father of a baby cannot deny a pregnant mother the right to abort if she chooses to do so, nor can he force her to undergo an abortion if she chooses not to do so.

- If the father of the baby wants to parent and the mother of the baby does not want to parent, she can legally release her rights to the father, and he can then have sole custody of the child.

There are important distinctions state-to-state—so it's important to find out what the law is in your area. A detailed list of these state laws can be found at www.childwelfare.gov.

When it comes to helping a teen mother decide what to do with the unborn baby, it's common for young boys initially at best to say, "I'll support whatever decision you choose," or at worst to pressure a girl to have an abortion. Sometimes this is because he is looking for a fast and easy solution, but often he is just parroting what he has heard on TV, or telling the girl what he thinks he is supposed to say. Teen boys, even more than girls, are disconnected about knowledge about conception, pregnancy, and the medical and emotional risks connected to an abortion.

Most medical pregnancy centers offer some form of male counseling for the father of the baby. The intent is to provide the young man with a trained individual who will educate and support him in the midst of the situation.

If the young girl chooses to parent the child, then your two families need to have some serious conversations about whether the teens will co-parent, and what your involvement as grandparents will be. Your son is on the edge of a steep learning curve for fatherhood. Talk to him about the type of father he wants to be and the type of role model he wants to be for his child. Encourage him to attend parenting classes and to seek out mentors and role models for this new season of his life.

Even if your son resists being an active father, you have the right as grandparents to be involved in your grandchild's life. Maintain a respect-ful, supportive relationship with the baby's mother and her family.

Although this pregnancy was a surprise, and probably not something you ever wanted, be encouraged! Many families have successfully navi-gated through these turbulent waters and have come out stronger on the other side. Concentrate on your family and the future well-being of your teen and their baby. Work together, support one another, and intention-ally create a plan that is truly in the best interest of everyone involved, including the unborn child.

PART 6: THE ELEPHANTS IN THE ROOM

We live in an increasingly complex world that challenges us every day with issues that can be difficult for teens to understand and for us to explain. And yet the most uncomfortable topics are often the most important ones to discuss.

Whenever I talk to parents about their tweens' and teens' sexuality, a number of related issues come up. In the following section I'll cover some of the most common—and most sensitive—topics that parents ask me about.

These chapters are short, and I don't always have clear-cut or easy solutions for you. The best thing you can do in every situation is to *not* ignore it, but to educate yourself and address it frankly with your teen.

Warning: the next few pages are going to get pretty graphic. As I stated above, I'm addressing some of the most common—and most sensitive—topics related to sexuality. One of the lessons that I've learned the hard way over the years of discussing such topics is they don't only apply to, or relate to, our teens. Many parents also need to address some of these questions on a personal level. After all, we are our teen's best examples, and the people they look to. If we are going to hold our teens to certain guidelines, the best way is to hold ourselves to the same standards.

14

MASTURBATION

We've established already that our teens are sexual beings, with human desires and curious hormones. They're surrounded by media and cultural messages that tell them that the purpose of sex is for pleasure. It's not terribly surprising, then, that after every parent meeting I facilitate, at least one parent, usually a mom, cautiously approaches me and asks, awkwardly, about masturbation.

This isn't just an issue that affects parents of boys. 23% of all teen girls fourteen to nineteen years old—and three-quarters of teen boys—report that they've masturbated at least once. A quarter of the girls and half of the boys masturbate at least twice a week.[79]

There are a lot of conflicting opinions about whether this is a normal, healthy, or even inevitable behavior. Where you stand as a parent will depend primarily on what you see as the purpose of sex. Is it just a tool for immediate personal pleasure? Or is it something deeper than that?

If we're going to counter the "hooking up" culture, then it's important to address the message that sexual activity is about more than instant, selfish gratification. Pure sex, in its deepest and most satisfying forms, brings two people together for bonding, mutual pleasure, and (sometimes) procreation. Sex is a mutual expression of love in marriage. Masturbation, which is sometimes called self-gratifying, doesn't fit into this vision.

On the surface, masturbation might seem like a harmless way to re-lease sexual temptation without the risk of sexual activity with another person. However, a study published in the *Archives of Pediatrics & Ado-lescent Medicine* found that teens who masturbate are more likely to have intercourse with a partner.[80] Like most secretive activities engaged in for selfish motives, there is a risk of addiction and long-term negative effects. A habit of compulsive masturbation can become an unhealthy substitution for future healthy sexual relationships within marriage or can become a symptom of other, larger sex addiction issues in which a person risks their health, relationships, and finances.

The secretive nature of masturbation also leads to short-term issues between parents and teens. Instinctively, teens have a fear of "getting caught" when they masturbate. They try to hide their behavior, which can lead to acting out or isolating themselves. Their fear often leads to guilt, which is confusing when they're surrounded by messages that self-gratification is okay...or even healthy!

So as awkward as the conversation may be, we need to take a deep breath and tackle this tough topic head on. Start to talk to your child as they enter puberty. If we're going to err, it's better to err on the side of bringing up the matter too soon rather than too late—chances are they've already heard about it in music, movies, and TV shows. Some compre-hensive sex education movements in public schools are even promoting masturbation as a healthy part of developing sexuality.

If you do walk in on your son or daughter masturbating, quickly turn away and/or leave the room to allow your teen privacy. Once everyone has recovered from the initial embarrassment, one parent needs to sit down with your teen and have a private, honest conversation. Ideally, this is a place for dads to speak to their sons and for moms to speak to their daughters, but if this isn't possible, don't let it keep you from having the conversation. Think through your approach in advance and choose your words carefully. Your goal here should not be to introduce more guilt or shame to the situation, but to educate your teen in a healthy man-ner about how to handle their feelings of curiosity, loneliness, boredom, and emptiness without giving in to temptations.

15

PORNOGRAPHY

Times have definitely changed our exposure to pornography. In the early 1950s, most stores didn't even carry pornography. In the 1960s, shops kept *Playboy* magazine out of sight behind the counter. In the 1970s, the racier *Penthouse* made it onto the shelf next to *Playboy*. Video stores in the '70s and '80s added "adult" sections. And then the Internet emerged in the '90s and took off in the twenty-first century, putting graphic depictions of sex just a mouse click away. Most teens today are exposed, at least accidentally or in passing, to a sexually explicit message or image. And that's a serious cause of concern for parents, who suspect—or know—that their child is consuming adult sexual content.

It's hard to get trustworthy, reliable statistics about the size and scale of the problem, partly because this is an industry that hides in the shadows, but mostly because the definitions of "pornography" aren't universal.

How do you define pornography? This isn't a trick question. I've talked to a lot of great, values-driven, committed parents in the past twenty years, and they've often drawn the lines of what's okay and what's not in different places. Some feel that romantic scenes in a movie, lingerie catalogs, explicit romance novels, and swimsuit issues of sports magazines are all forms of porn. Some see nude art pieces in museums and public places as indecent and inappropriate. Others limit their concern to what we've classically called "porn": adult movies, magazines, and websites.

In the past few years, some concerned writers have started to describe what's been termed "emotional pornography." Science tells us that teen boys are more likely than girls to be aroused by visual stimuli like photos and movies. But that doesn't mean that teen girls don't struggle with unrealistic images. Teen girls are more easily aroused by romantic fantasies.[81] While *visual pornography* stimulates the body with explicitly sexual images or words, *emotional pornography* stimulates a person's idealistic and emotional sense of romance and adventure. According to this perspective, romantic movies like *The Notebook* and *Twilight* are just as dangerous as the Victoria's Secret catalog, because they engage an unrealistic image of a fairy tale romance.

Either way, the result is a warped view of reality that can leave the participant struggling to reconcile a false image with a real person.

The saddest, most damaging effect of pornography is that it objectifies people—separating the personality and soul of a person from their body and making them an object rather than a unique and complex creation. Porn trains its viewers to believe in a version of reality that does not actually exist. Marketers and producers provide instant and exaggerated gratification to the desires of men and women, dehumanizing participants and spectators alike. Women are the victims of this demeaning perspective more often than not, but porn is equal opportunity, and there are plenty of men who are lured into the lifestyle of porn. Pornography addiction dehumanizes women and desensitizes men's view of them. A pornography addiction creates serious issues for real-world intimacy and can be a huge problem for intimacy within marriage. Marital sex, over the long term, cannot compete with the intensity of porn.

The effects of a pornography addiction—or even experimentation—cannot be overstated. It is full of appealing but misguided messages about the power dynamics between partners and what defines normal behavior—not just sexual behavior but relational behavior as well.

How do we practically prepare our teens to confront the difficult temptations of visual and emotional pornography—and the problems of addiction that pornography can so often lead to? Like most of the topics we've looked at in this book, it begins with these broadly identified suggestions and open, honest communication:

- **Be clear:** Before you can tackle the issue of pornography with your tween and teen, it's important for you and your spouse, if appropriate, to sit down and determine what you consider "pornographic," inappropriate material for your son or daughter. Parents need to identify the boundaries before their children can know and hopefully obey the boundaries.

- **Be proactive:** Ignoring pornography and leaving it in the shadows won't work. Porn producers aren't sitting back and waiting for your teen to find them; they're actively recruiting and advertising to young people. Don't wait for your teen to come to you with questions about pornography. They need you to talk to them about what they're seeing elsewhere, so help them understand that pornography is a path that produces extreme issues. Sit down and talk to your teen maturely and with compassion.

- **Be prepared:** While plenty of pornographic material is still being printed and distributed the old-fashioned way, Internet pornography is the fastest-growing segment...and the easiest for our teens to access. It's important for you to educate yourself about the various technology tools in your home—not just the family desktop but also your teen's laptop, tablet, or smart phone. How can they access the Internet? Where are the video and still cameras that can upload pictures? Research options for monitoring and safeguarding your teen's Internet access; there are dozens of services and software available today.

- **Be patient:** This is where many parents struggle the most. If you discover that your son or daughter has been experimenting with pornography, it's important to not react emotionally or try to shame your teen. Show compassion and strength rather than frustration and anger. There's a chance that your daughter or son is moving toward an addiction issue, which is serious and needs to be addressed. Punishing without relationship and support in that case won't work. If you are faced with this sort of situation, seek out the support of a counselor who specializes in this area and can help your teen unpack their reasons for experimenting with pornography. The goal is to develop a plan for how to move forward in a healthy manner. No matter what, don't give up on your teen.

- **Be diligent:** One of the challenges of pornography is that it is free, easily available, comes in multiple formats, and is accessible twenty-four hours a day. Physical or emotional stimulation is just a click away all day long. This creates challenges for you, the parent, as well as a challenge for your son or daughter. Do everything you can to support your teen by removing their access to porn: move the desktop computer into a family area where the screen is visible; set expectations for when personal tablets, phones, and laptops need to be powered down for the night and left in a public place; and monitor your teen's web habits.

Pornography addiction is real, and it is vying for the hearts and souls of our young men and women. Be on the lookout for signs of weakness for the sake of your teen daughter or son. If they are weak in this area, let them know how courageous they are, encourage them to move away from the temptations. Ensure them their problem with porn does not define their value, that they are your child and your love for them doesn't fluctuate based on when they are succeeding in this area or when they are losing this battle. Intentionally help them to find the resources they need for the journey.

Here are additional resources to help you dig deeper if you believe this is an area you need assistance with:

- http://fightthenewdrug.org/

16

SEXTING

M ost teens today document their entire lives online through social media. They don't think twice about sharing silly or embarrassing photos, thoughtless or immature comments, and what seems to parents like strings of random letters.

JK LOL IDK RU?

Huh?

They have grown up believing they should be "on" and available at all times, regardless of the psychological cost. And when it comes to sexting, there's a heavy psychological cost.

When teens take and send sexually revealing pictures of themselves or send sexually explicit text messages, it's called "sexting." Kids "sext" to show off, to entice someone, to show interest in someone, or to prove commitment. It's one of the most obvious displays of the developing teen mind's impulsiveness and inability to think through potential consequences. And the sad news is, sexting is a teen reality that's probably here to stay.

As concerning as it is to think about a teen sending a pornographic image of themselves to another person they know, the real risk is that they've now let that image out into cyberspace. There's no way to control who will see it or how widely it will be shared.

It is rare that a "sext" message or photo remains private between the sender and the intended receiver. This was obvious in the case of Cincinnati teen Jesse Logan, who in 2008 committed suicide after a nude photo she'd sent to a boyfriend was circulated widely around her high school, resulting in harassment from her classmates.[82] In 2013, a high school athletic director in Evanston, Illinois, made headlines when he pulled his school's baseball team out of the regional playoffs after discovering that the players had been sharing nude images of girls received via sexting.[83]

When it comes to understanding the intersection of cyberspace and personal boundaries, one of the most important messages we can share with our tweens and teens is that there's no such thing as control of information in a world where anything can be copied, sent, posted, and seen by huge audiences. As soon as they *take the photo*, before they even hit "send," they have created a personal risk. Their intentions don't matter.

Every teen should approach their electronic communications, from photos to emails, with the idea that the very last person they would ever want to see that photo—whether that's the most popular girl in school or the meanest bully or their pastor or *you*—may see it. Are they prepared for that? If not, it's best to leave the camera off and the words off the screen.

Furthermore, sending sexual images to minors is against the law, and some states have begun prosecuting teens for child pornography or felony obscenity for sending photos of nude minors to others in their schools or friend groups.[84]

Don't wait for an incident to happen to your teen or one of your teen's friends before you talk about the consequences of sexting. As soon as your tween or teen has their first cell phone or social media account, make sure they know how to handle it. Help them make the connection between peer pressure/bullying and sexting. Most teens—especially girls—who sext images of themselves report that they did it because someone asked them to. Make it clear that no matter how intense the social pressure is, the potential social humiliation will most definitely be worse.

On the other side, as bullying increasingly moves into the cyberspace world, it's also important for your son or daughter to know what to do if they receive an embarrassing or explicit photo of someone else. In today's teen culture, where approximately 93% of young people have access to some form of social media and the "send to all" button is so easy to hit, most teens will face unsolicited sexually explicit pictures or videos of a person they know or are somehow connected to.

The primary guideline is always to delete immediately, and if it continues, or if it seems like there is a situation that is putting someone into emotional or physical harm, they need to tell a trusted adult right away. Suicide among bullied teens is a serious issue.

Not all sexting happens among innocent, if misguided, teens. "Sextortion" happens when a person—which might be a pornography producer or other adult in the sex industry or might be a teen peer—acquires a nude or seminude photograph or video of another person and then uses that photograph or video to blackmail, intimidate, or exploit the person in the picture. There have been cases where teens were unknowingly videotaped during online chats with friends, or had their pictures taken in the locker room in a state of half-dress, and then these pictures and videos were passed around.

The rise of sextortion has turned peers into predators, and the offenders are getting younger. In 2014, a thirteen-year-old boy in Virginia was charged with blackmailing as many as six girls into performing sex acts by threatening to forward their sexted images to his friends.[85]

Tweens and young teens are especially vulnerable to sextortion because their embarrassment and shame overpowers other emotions. They worry about how their parents will react or think that if they tell someone that the embarrassing image will just spread further. They are often rarely mature enough to recognize that they are a victim of a sex crime.

Unfortunately, the sheer nature of sextortion—happening out of sight, on mobile phones and private social media profiles—makes protecting our teens infinitely more challenging. If you've ever had an uncomfortable talk with your kids about sex, or watched them blush at even the mere word of it, you can imagine how uncomfortable a discussion about sextortion might make them feel. Regardless, help your teen stay safe by following these widely used guidelines:

- **Talk with your teen about sexting and sextortion.** Define both. Answer any questions they may have in reference to it. Reinforce that it is illegal to be taking, sending, or even receiving sexually revealing pictures and videos of someone under the age of seventeen (even if the teen themselves took the photo).

- **Stay connected to your teen's online presence.** We keep discussing this, but as we shared earlier, it's a non-negotiable. It will be time consuming, given the amount of time that kids are online, but it's critical. Insist on knowing all of your teen's accounts, and create your own to stay connected. (If your teen is on Facebook, you should have your own Facebook profile. If they're on Instagram, have an Instagram account of your own.) Stay connected to your teen as their friend/follower/etc. Regularly check in to see not just what they're saying but what others are saying to them.

- **Be sure your teen understands** that obtaining something, like photos, or getting someone to act in a certain way via social networking—through the use of force or threats is illegal. Demanding sex acts from a minor is also a criminal act.

- **Have an agreement with your teen** that the only way they are allowed to have social networking accounts, which includes their cell phone pictures and videos, is if you have access to their passwords. Be sure that the agreement explains that you will only do an assessment of their private messages if you see something that concerns you. As the adult, don't take advantage of this; teens deserve a certain amount of privacy, and if they feel like you're always "snooping," they're likely to just get better at hiding things. You're only looking for the big, life-altering things.

The most important thing, though, is to keep talking and to do it in a nonconfrontational way. Help your teen see that you're not accusing them of anything wrong, nor are you trying to shame them away from normal, friendly interaction online. In every situation, remind your teen that you are their ally and not their enemy.

17

SEXUAL ABUSE AND SEXUAL ASSAULT

A NEW story seems to hit the news every week:

- A high school football season is cancelled after senior players sexually assault members of the freshman team, justifying it as "hazing."[86]

- A high school teacher is arrested for sexually assaulting his children's babysitter while his wife sleeps in the next room.[87]

- A high-profile, highly respected college football coach is convicted of sexually abusing dozens of young men he was supposed to be mentoring. The abuse went on for decades, and school officials were indicted for covering up and failing to report the abuse.[88]

I could fill pages with stories like this. Our teens are growing up in a dangerous world, where sexual assault is a serious risk. The numbers are staggering:

- One in four girls are sexually abused by the age of eighteen.

- One in six boys are sexually abused by the age of eighteen.

- Most teen sexual abuse victims (70%) know their abuser.

- Teenagers account for 51% of all reported sexual abuse.

- Teenagers between the ages of sixteen and nineteen are three-and-a-half times more likely than the general public to be victims of sexual abuse.

- 23% of all sexual offenders are under the age of eighteen.[89]

I don't share these statistics to scare you. As parents, we can't hide our heads in the sand about this issue, though. We need to prepare our teens to be responsible, empowered, and bold in speaking out. Sex offenders—both adults and other teenagers—look for victims who can be convinced to stay quiet about inappropriate physical contact.

Start by making sure your tween or teen knows how to recognize inappropriate touching or advances. Simply stated, if *anyone* touches them in their private areas—what we've been calling the underwear zone—that is not okay. It doesn't matter who that person is or what the person says to them; they need to tell you, or another trusted adult, immediately.

Many teens don't tell anyone about sexual assault because they're embarrassed or erroneously think that they did something to "deserve" the treatment. Reinforce that your teen will not get in trouble if they tell you they've been touched inappropriately. It doesn't matter if they made questionable decisions, like going to a party or ignoring other advances or wearing something revealing, before that. Nothing they do can ever justify another person sexually assaulting them. Let them know that you will always believe them, help them, and love them.

IF YOUR TEEN HAS BEEN ASSAULTED

If your teen comes to you and shares that any kind of inappropriate contact has happened to them, the most important thing you can do in that moment is to listen more than you talk. Avoid asking a lot of questions right away. They may need time to process through the details, and your first priority is to not appear to blame or doubt their story in any way.

If the assault just happened, you need to go to a doctor or emergency room *immediately* to record any evidence. Difficult as it may be, it's important that the victim does *not* shower and does *not* throw away the clothes worn at the time of the incident. Physical evidence from the assault needs to be gathered first.

If your son or daughter tells you about an incident that happened in the past, contact a counselor who specializes in child sexual abuse and who can help your teen privately work through the situation and begin the healing process. You will probably benefit from some counseling as well. The counselor can help your family make a plan for reporting the situation to the correct authority.

Reporting any incident of sexual assault—from rape to inappropriate touching—is an emotionally difficult, but critical, step. For many victims and their families, going to the authorities makes the abuse "real" because it's public. But if you do not report the incident, or if you delay reporting, the offender is left to potentially perpetrate sexual abuse against other victims, and your family is left with the situation unresolved.

Most states have mandatory reporting laws on known or suspected sexual abuse. Educate yourself, ask questions, take a step back, and privately process through a plan that is in your family's best interest.

Here are additional resources to help you dig deeper if you believe this is an area you need assistance with:

- https://www.rainn.org/get-help/national-sexual-assault-hotline

SEX TRAFFICKING

When we hear about sex trafficking, the images that come to mind are usually from far away countries: destitute families in dusty villages who sell their daughters into prostitution or smarmy pimps who offer tourists illicit exploits with children.

Sadly, that's not the case. There is an active sex trafficking industry in the United States, and it's targeting teens from all classes. Organizations who rescue underage and coerced sex workers report that victims come from the middle-class suburbs as well as the inner cities.

There are several different scenarios that lead a teen into the sex trade. Predators offer false connections, promising a future of modeling agencies or global travel. Or a pimp will act like a loving boyfriend, acting as a knight in shining armor and building a dependent relationship, until he forces her to be "turned out." Or an adult will "rescue" a teen in crisis and offer safety—for a price.

There are a number of common risk factors for young boys and girls who could become victims of sexual exploitation:

- Conflicts at home

- Getting kicked out of the home

- Parental neglect

- Physical or sexual abuse

- Homelessness

- Poverty

- Educational failure

- Emotional problems like low self-esteem

- Social isolation from their peers (the "outcasts" and loners)

- Running away

As with every other issue discussed in this book, education and awareness are key factors in protecting your teens. Be aware of who their friends are, who they're communicating with online, and make your teen is aware of the problem. The most vulnerable teens are those who are not informed and are therefore more susceptible to false promises.

Discuss the risks, discuss the scenarios, and make sure your teen knows exactly who they can trust (and who they can't).

Here are additional resources to help you dig deeper if you believe this is an area you need assistance with:

- http://www.state.gov/j/tip/id/domestic/index.htm

- http://www.polarisproject.org/

- http://www.a21.org/index.php

18

ALCOHOL

Teen drinking is nothing new. Chances are, you knew about a few teen parties when you were in school. Yet as parents, it's a whole different experience when our fifteen-year-old comes stumbling through the front door with beer on her breath or when the police call because our seventeen-year-old was at an underage party that was raided.

Young people who drink are more likely to engage in at-risk sexual activity and have multiple sex partners. Some researchers speculate that a teenager's desire for sexual pleasure far outreaches their capacity for solid and sound decision making. In other words, teens are more vulnerable to addiction because the pleasure center of the brain matures to adult proportions well before the part of the brain responsible for impulse control and executive decision making.[90] To provide perspective, if a teen consumes their first drink of alcohol at age fourteen or younger, they will be six times more likely to develop alcohol related issues than those who don't try alcohol until the legal drinking age.[91]

The National Youth Risk Behavior Survey states the following:[92]

- One-third of high school students (38.7%) report drinking alcohol.

- One in five teens (21.9%) report binge drinking (five or more drinks of alcohol within a couple of hours).

- One in five teens (20.5%) report that they first tried alcohol (more than a few sips) for the first time before age thirteen.

Alcohol is the most commonly used and abused drug among youth in the United States, more than tobacco and illicit drugs. When I talk to teens about the connections between alcohol consumption and sexual activity, they justify their partying in a few different ways:

- Teen drinking is okay as long as I don't get caught.

- Teen drinking is okay as long as I don't drink and drive.

- Teen drinking is okay as long as I don't get drunk.

- Teen drinking is okay as long as I don't die.

The disturbing thing is that there are plenty of parents who feel the same way. They see drinking as something inevitable, or a rite of passage, and so they don't do anything to prevent it. "I did it when I was their age" is an argument I hear often, even from parents who are otherwise committed to helping their children stay safe. Some parents even have the attitude that "if I provide them with alcohol and a safe place to drink it, they'll learn moderation."

Yet the opposite is usually true. Studies show that adolescents whose parents allow them moderate amounts of alcohol are actually more likely to drink outside their parents' influence, and to drink more than their peers.[93] This increases their risks of other poor behavior choices and dangerous outcomes among their peers.

THE TEEN PARTY SCENE

There are many different scenarios for sexual assault and nonconsensual sexual advances, but in the teen world, alcohol is a common factor. According to a study of college students done by Brown University:

- 55% of female students and 75% of male students involved in acquaintance rape admit to having been drinking or using drugs when the incident occurred.

- 90% of all campus rapes occur when alcohol has been used by either the assailant or the victim.

- As many as 70% of college students admit to having engaged in sexual activity primarily as a result of being under the influence of alcohol or to having sex they wouldn't have had if they had been sober.[94]

Even teens who have personally committed to not drinking or taking drugs might struggle with peer pressure in environments where alcohol and drugs are freely passed around. Or, even more frightening, they may continue to abstain but become a victim of someone whose inhibitions are dulled.

When your teen reaches the age where parties are happening among their peers, make sure they understand three basic guidelines:

1. Don't present yourself as a victim. If they attend a party or event where teens are drinking or doing drugs, there are things your teen can do to lessen their chances of being assaulted.

   - Be aware of "date rape drugs." Rohypnol, GHB, ecstasy, and ketamine are easy to hide, colorless, and odorless. They act as depressants or hallucinogens and leave their victims unable to respond or react to what's happening around—or to—them.[95] If your teen is in a social setting, they should never let anyone else pour their drink—even if it's water or something non-alcoholic. Don't trust a "punch bowl"—it's too easy for anyone to slip something into it. They should always open their own drinks, preferably single-serving cans or bottles, and never leave their drink unattended. Stay where others can see you. Train your teen not to go off alone with another person into any setting that's away from the group (a bedroom, a walk down a deserted beach, someone's empty house, a parked car). This is especially true if the person is a stranger or is intoxicated. Remind your teen that if they are ever in a situation that's not safe, they can contact you, and you will immediately come and get them, no questions asked.

   - Be prepared. If your teen is going to a party, have a transportation plan in place. Who is the designated driver? When teens get a driver's license, teach them to keep their car doors locked and to have a plan for personal defense if they are assaulted (for example, self-defense training or martial arts, a siren or alarm on their keychain, or, in areas where it's legal, a canister of pepper spray or other chemical deterrent).

2. Don't get carried away. Alcohol can lower a teen's inhibitions. As more stories emerge across the country about dangerous parties and tragic consequences, there is sometimes an attitude that "boys will be boys." Entire communities have been accused of excusing popular students and athletes ("They couldn't help it") or even blaming the victim ("Did you see what she was wearing?"). It's up to you to train your teen that these kind of attitudes are never acceptable. If your teen decides to drink or act in a way that lowers their inhibitions, they are still entirely responsible for their actions. If they are part of a group of friends who "get carried away," their behavior is still criminal and will be punished. Any kind of sexual activity requires the voluntary consent of both parties. A teen is not capable of consent if they are unconscious, asleep, or intoxicated.

3. Don't be a bystander. In too many stories of sexual assault at a teen party, there are bystanders who see what's happening and don't do anything to stop it or report it. With the above points in mind, talk to your teen about their personal responsibility if they see another person being violated or put in a dangerous position.

   • Don't leave a person who appears to be impaired alone or isolated. Often sexual assault at a party is a crime of opportunity, and all it takes is the presence of another person to dissuade the potential perpetrator.

   • Speak up. If your teen sees something happening that is wrong, encourage them to be an advocate for the victim. This can be hard for teens, who are generally concerned with not drawing negative peer attention, but is a symbol of their character. If anyone starts pulling out a phone to record a person who is not in control of their actions, it's time to step in.

During your son or daughter's teen years, as a parent, you have a major impact on the choices that they makes. Researchers state that family rituals such as keeping daily routines and celebrating holidays together steers teenagers away from using and abusing alcohol. One study shares that tweens and teens who grow up in homes with alcohol issues already present will be less likely to abuse alcohol themselves if they learn solid coping skill, live in an organized environment, and feel some sense of control during their daily life.[96]

Talking openly and honestly about drinking is vitally important. Delaying the age at which your teen takes their first drink lowers their risk of becoming problem drinkers. That's reason enough to talk to your teen daughter or son about alcohol, but it's not the only one, drinking interferes with good judgment, leading to risky behavior and making them vulnerable to sexual coercion, and it's illegal.

19

SEXUAL ORIENTATION

IT DOESN'T matter whether I am speaking to parents at a private paro-chial school or a public school in the city. Almost always, after I present the Pure Sexual Freedom model, a mom or dad waits until the room clears and everyone has started leaving. They'll approach me cau-tiously, hem and haw, and then finally tell me their story. Inevitably, they are concerned because their son or daughter has announced that they are gay or are questioning their orientation. They often look to me with a desperate plea to "fix" their situation or solve what they see as a serious problem.

The flip side of this story is the fact that at the exact same parent meeting, there are often parents of a son or daughter who has come out of the closet and is thriving. Those families are fully accepting and feel no reason to be concerned.

This is one of the toughest and most controversial questions I am faced with—and one which I am not fully equipped to answer. Remem-ber, I'm the mother of three straight daughters. I spend my days working with teens who are concerned about unplanned pregnancy—something that's the result of heterosexual sex.

Ten years ago, while teaching sexual health, I don't remember any-one ever questioning me about same sex relationships. Today, I regularly speak to classes where students are open about questioning their sexual-ity, or are quite explicit about being gay or lesbian.

COMMON TERMS RELATED TO SEXUAL ORIENTATION

The following terms have become part of the common vocabulary in our country—and likely are or will become part of your son or daughter's vocabulary as well:

- **Sexual Orientation:** A person's natural sexual attraction

- **Heterosexual/Straight:** A person who is sexually attracted to members of the opposite sex

- **Homosexual/Gay:** A person who is sexually attracted to members of one's own sex (applies to both males and females)

- **Lesbian:** A female who is sexually attracted to only females

- **Bisexual:** A person who is sexually responsive to both sexes

- **Bi-curious:** A heterosexual person who wonders about/experiments sexually with members of the same sex

- **Asexual:** A person who experiences no sexual desire for either gender

- **Queer:** This term is used in differing ways, depending on who uses it and for what purpose. Sometimes it is used negatively, as a slur against someone perceived as homosexual or who has openly identified themselves as gay. Other times it is used positively by openly gay individuals as a term to describe going against social norms.

There are a lot of complicated ideas here to unpack, but for now, let's focus on an awareness that the culture has shifted drastically and quickly regarding sexual orientation and behavior. Fifty years ago, homosexual activity was actually illegal in most states. Today, gay couples have the legal rights to marry and raise children, a change that is based largely on the changing attitudes of younger generations.[97] What was kept in the shadows when most of us were growing up is now shining in the spotlights, some families are thrilled it's out in the open and some families are trying to learn how to live in this new reality.

Despite the cultural shift, most tweens and teens identify as heterosexual. Those who don't, or who are starting to question their sexuality, often share with me that they are facing immense social and emotional challenges, like being bullied, depression, and verbal and physical assaults.

There are still debates, contrasting studies, and conflicting personal values and morals surrounding the issues of sexual orientation, and it's possible there always will be. Every family needs to work through this carefully and thoughtfully, and to help their teen know how to do the same.

WHERE TO BEGIN?

Think back to the months before you brought your first child home and began the parenting season of life. Do you remember everything you did: all the advice you solicited, the books you read, the preparations you made, the beautiful dreams you composed in your head for how their lives would unfold?

A family with questions about their son or daughter's orientation often experiences a similar season of uncertainty and fear of the unknown. You may have moments of worry and doubt. Your son or daughter's future no longer looks the way you may have imagined it.

If you are experiencing this type of situation, it's natural to feel overwhelmed. But in the midst of this natural feeling, there's one nonnegotiable point that needs to be remembered.

First, foremost, and above all: **your son or daughter needs to know that you love them**. Period. Your teen is more than their sexual orientation or their sexual behavior. A teen who feels like their parent is trying to judge, change, or blame them risks feeling rejected, abandoned, or isolated and may turn to others for acceptance. Now, more than ever, they need your steady love. In the middle of your own doubts and difficulties, passionately love your daughter or son and do everything you can to assure them that the love is unwavering.

In addition to loving your son or daughter, consider these points to help you reset your thoughts for what the future holds.[98]

- **Remember, all teen sexual activity is dangerous.** The principles communicated throughout this book apply to your son or daughter regardless of their sexual orientation. All teens, heterosexual and homosexual, need to be educated and understand that they can choose to protect themselves from long-term consequences and health risks by choosing not to engage in at-risk sexual activity. For the sake of review, the *physical risks* from sexual activity start well before intercourse, when a person *touches any part of another person's body that is normally covered by underwear*, which includes skin-to-skin contact, and/or *any time body fluids come into contact with body openings.*

- **Fix your heart securely to your sleeve.** Make no mistake—there are awkward, messy, tearful, painful conversations ahead. Fully commit to having them. The greatest gift you can give your son or daughter right now is to offer them the same soul-baring honesty they have given you. Show them the great humility of admitting that you don't understand and also the deep compassion that you want to understand. Come clean about your questions and your inability to grasp so much about this, but be relentless in reminding them that you want to walk alongside them.

- **If you believe in prayer, pray.** Right now you might be tempted to pray that God will "fix" or change your son or daughter. Is that possible? There's nothing God can't do, so yes. Is it likely? I don't know. But regardless, pray that God will work in and around and through each member of your family as you navigate through this season of uncertainty. Pray that you can identify blessings in the midst of the challenges.

- **Become a student.** One of the most difficult parts of being a parent and adult is admitting when we're at the limit of what we know and understand. Chances are, you already have some very specific and passionate ideas about homosexuality. Some are a product of your upbringing and some are simply a product of the adult life you've lived and what you have or haven't been exposed to. Do your best to put those aside and become a willing student of sexual orientation. Select your teachers wisely and learn everything you can about sexuality, the human body, the Lesbian, Gay, Bisexual, Transgender (LGBT) culture, and your teen. Ask the difficult questions. Learn things you don't yet know. Boldly process through the information you gather and challenge yourself to identify what you consider to be true and what you consider to be false, what you consider to be helpful and what you consider to be harmful and hurtful.

- **Realize that you'll be in or out of the closet as a family.** One of the most difficult decisions you'll make as this journey unfolds is who to share this news with. It can be difficult and stressful to choose who you can trust with this intimate part of your lives, because this is a family situation. If you decide to be "out" with your teen's sexuality, you will be "out" as a family. If you live in a community that treats homosexuality with an unfair stigma, you may face the same judgment, discrimination, and pushback that your daughter or son does. Likewise, if you choose to keep your child's sexual orientation hidden, you, too, will experience the strain of keeping part of you hidden, and the internal struggle of partial honesty with people around you.

- **Remember you are still Mom and Dad to your son or daughter.** Your teen may look different to you as a result of what they've shared about their sexuality, but it's important to realize that they haven't changed their perception of you. You're still the most influential people in their lives—the ones they look up to and turn to and seek approval from and refuge in. Do all the things that you did before you discovered their hidden reality: spend time with your kids, attend their games and events, help with their homework, pester them to clean their rooms and eat healthier food and get off the computer. Go on vacations, go out to dinner, go shopping. Continue to be a family in as many normal, ordinary, routine ways as you can, because the wonderful reality is that you are a family. Don't postpone your home life or your family's future until you reach some decision or get some clarity. Your kids are

growing up now, and the precious, fleeting days you have with
them are happening as we speak. Be a family!

- **Don't quit.** Even if you feel like you're losing your relationship
  with your teen, have hope; the way things are right now is not the
  way things will always be. Just like any difficult event, there is
  no substitute for time. You will grow and learn and come to understand things. The rawness and urgency of these days will fade,
  and the jagged edges of uncertainty will soften, but for now, there's
  no way around this. You simply have to do the dirty, unpleasant,
  uncomfortable work of getting up every day and living.

Yes, this is a complicated subject for some, and one that may be difficult for you and your family to process through. I recommend that you
find a counselor that specializes in teen sexual orientation, who can help
both you and your daughter or son process through their questions and
concerns in a confidential, safe, and supportive environment. Given the
deeply contrasting perspectives that surround this topic, do your homework when selecting a counselor and make sure the counselor you select
is in line with your family's values and beliefs.

CONCLUSION

TEENS today are under tremendous pressure to be sexually active. Regardless, parents, stay the course! Be diligent. Model healthy relationships, and love your children generously through these difficult years. Provide them with solid standards that will equip them to live a healthy life. Nurture the parent-teen relationship with rich family experiences.

There are no easy solutions for parents when it comes to tackling the tough issue of teen sexual activity. The longer I'm a parent and the older our three daughters become, the more I'm aware of the depth of the issue.

Teens hear advice on all kinds of issues from their parents, teachers, and other adults in their lives, but we rarely ask them to offer advice to us. So I want to leave you with their words, not mine.

We asked teens, "If you could give your parents and other important adults in your life advice about how to help you and your friends avoid teen sex, what would it be?" These were the top ten things we heard:

- *Show* us why teen sexual activity is so unhealthy. Don't just lecture us and expect us to take your word for it. Let us hear directly from other teens about their experiences. Even though most of us don't think it will happen to us, sometimes we need real-life examples to help us understand how often it does happen.

- **Honestly talk to us about relationships, sex, and love.** Just because we're young doesn't mean we're not capable of falling in love.

Our feelings are very real and powerful to us. Help us learn how to handle them without getting hurt or hurting others, instead of wishing we didn't have the feelings.

- **Telling us not to have sex is not enough.** Explain why we shouldn't have sex and ask us what we think. Tell us how you felt as a teen. Listen to us and take our opinions seriously. And no lectures, please!

- **Whether we're having sex or not, we need to be prepared.** We need to know how to avoid peer pressure situations related to sex.

- **If we ask you about sex, don't assume we are already "doing it."** Maybe we're just curious, or maybe we want to talk with someone we trust. Don't assume that giving us information about sex will encourage us to have sex.

- **Pay attention to us** *before* **we get into trouble.** Programs for teen moms and teen fathers are great, but we all need encouragement, attention, and support. Reward us for doing the right thing, even when it seems like no big deal.

- **Sometimes, all it takes not to have sex is not to have the opportunity.** Don't leave us alone so much. If you can't be home with us after school, make sure we have something to do that we really like, where there are other kids around and adults who are good leaders and good role models. Often we end up having sex because there's not much else to do.

- **We really care what you think, even if we don't act like it.** When we don't end up doing exactly what you tell us to, don't think that you've failed to reach us. Instead, talk about how to do better the next time.

- **Show us what good, responsible relationships look like.** We're influenced as much by what you do as by what you say. If you demonstrate healthy communication and responsibility in your own relationships, we'll be more likely to follow your example.

- **We hate "The Talk" as much as you do.** Instead, begin talking with us about sex and responsibility when we're young, and keep the conversation going as we grow older. This will make it a lot easier to talk about when we experience things in our social environment that don't make sense.

NOTES

[1]National Center for HIV/AIDS, Viral Hepatitis, STD, and TB Prevention, *Trends in the Prevalence of Sexual Behaviors and HIV Testing: National YRBS: 1991-2011*, accessed January 31, 2015, http://www.cdc.gov/healthyyouth/yrbs/pdf/us_sexual_trend_yrbs.pdf.

[2]University of Plymouth, "New Link in Obesity in Young, Lowering of Age of Puberty," *Science Daily*, accessed January 31, 2015, http://www.sciencedaily.com/releases/2014/07/140728094451.htm.

[3]Carey Wallace, "3 Reasons Your Daughter's Puberty Won't Be Like Yours," *Time*, January 9, 2015, http://time.com/3659760/3-reasons-your-daughters-puberty-wont-be-like-yours/.

[4]Tim Elmore, "The Marks of Maturity," *Psychology Today* (blog), November 12, 2012, https://www.psychologytoday.com/blog/artificial-maturity/201211/the-marks-maturity.

[5]Irving DeJohn, "3 Teens Admit to Attacking Audrie Pott, Leading Her to Commit Suicide," *The New York Daily News*, January 15, 2014, http://www.nydailynews.com/news/national/audrie-pott-attackers-admit-attack-caused-commit-suicide-article-1.1580284.

[6]Guttmacher Institute, *American Teens' Sexual and Reproductive Health*, fact sheet, May 2014, http://www.guttmacher.org/pubs/FB-ATSRH.html.

[7]Dennis Rainey, "Aggressive Girls, Clueless Boys," *Family Life*, accessed January 31, 2015,

http://www.familylife.com/articles/topics/parenting/essentials/raising-boys/aggressive-girls-clueless-boys\#.VM0Y9GjF-So.

[8]Lawrence B. Finer and Jesse M. Philbin, "Sexual Initiation, Contraceptive Use, and Pregnancy among Young Adolescents," *Pediatrics* 131, no. 5(2013), http://pediatrics.aappublications.org/content/early/2013/03/27/peds.2012-3495.

[9]Kendra Cherry, "Parenting Styles: The Four Style of Parenting," About.com, accessed January 31, 2015, http://psychology.about.com/od/developmentalpsychology/a/parenting-style.htm.

[10]National Center for HIV/AIDS, Viral Hepatitis, STD, and TB Prevention, *Trends in the Prevalence of Sexual Behaviors and HIV Testing: National YRBS: 1991-2011*, accessed January 31, 2015, http://www.cdc.gov/healthyyouth/yrbs/pdf/us_sexual_trend_yrbs.pdf.

[11]Bill Peter, *Role Modeling and Parenting*, (publisher unknown), http://globalinnovationfoundation.org/uploaded/Doc/role_modeling_and_parenting_c0813a.pdf.

[12]"Inside the Teenage Brain," *Frontline* (PBS, January 31, 2002), television program, http://www.pbs.org/wgbh/pages/frontline/shows/teenbrain/view/.

[13]Jane Anderson, "The Teenage Brain: Under Construction," American College of Pediatricians, May 2011, https://www.acpeds.org/the-college-speaks/position-statements/parenting-issues/the-teenage-brain-under-construction.

[14]*Dictionary.com*, s.v. "critical thinking," accessed May 31, 2014, http://dictionary.reference.com/browse/criticalthinking.

[15]Jane Anderson, "The Teenage Brain: Under Construction," American College of Pediatricians, May 2011, https://www.acpeds.org/the-college-speaks/position-statements/parenting-issues/the-teenage-brain-under-construction.

[16]Dr. Dave Walsh, "Experience Counts: Development of the Brain – Part 1," *Mind Positive Parenting* (blog), May 19, 2011, http://drdavewalsh.com/posts/57.

[17]Wikipedia "Maslow's hierarchy of needs," accessed March 13, 2015,

http://en.wikipedia.org/wiki/Maslow\%27s_hierarchy_of_needs.

[18]Centers for Disease Control and Prevention, *Condoms and STDs: Fact Sheet for Public Health Personnel*, fact sheet, last modified March 25, 2013, http://www.cdc.gov/condomeffectiveness/latex.html.

[19]The National Campaign to Prevent Teen and Unplanned Pregnancy, *Fast Facts: Teen Pregnancy in the United States*, fact sheet, August 2014, http://thenationalcampaign.org/sites/default/files/resource-primary-download/fast_facts_-_teen_pregnancy_in_the_united_states_aug_2014_0.pdf.

[20]"Teen Pregnancy: Medical Risks and Realities," Web MD, accessed March 1, 2015, http://www.webmd.com/baby/guide/teen-pregnancy-medical-risks-and-realities?page=2.

[21]World Health Organization, *Sexually Transmitted Infections (STIs)*, fact sheet no. 110, November 2013, http://www.who.int/mediacentre/factsheets/fs110/en/.

[22]Centers for Disease Control and Prevention, Information for Teens: Staying Healthy and Preventing STDs, fact sheet, November 4, 2014, http://www.cdc.gov/std/life-stages-populations/stdfact-teens.htm.

[23]Centers for Disease Control and Prevention, "Nationally Representative CDC Study Finds 1 in 4 Teenage Girls Has a Sexually Transmitted Disease," news release, March 11, 2008, http://www.cdc.gov/stdconference/2008/press/release-11march2008.htm.

[24]World Health Organization, *Sexually Transmitted Infections (STIs)*, fact sheet no. 110, November 2013, http://www.who.int/mediacentre/factsheets/fs110/en/.

[25]"What Is a Sexually Transmitted Infection (STI)?" Northern Territory Government, Australia, March 1, 2015, http://www.safesexnoregrets.nt.gov.au/sti.html.

[26]http://www.cdc.gov/std/life-stages-populations/stdfact-teens.htm

[27]Haley Checkley, "Controversy Condemning Gardasil May Be Warranted," *The Exponent*, last modified November 6, 2014, http://www.purdueexponent.org/features/article_209898d8-1f65-596d-8f12-8cfc6938bde4.html.

[28]"HPV Vaccines," Centers for Disease Control and Prevention, last modified January 26, 2015, http://www.cdc.gov/hpv/vaccine.html.

[29] Robert Rector, Kirk A. Johnson, and Lauren R. Noyes, "Sexually Active Teenagers Are More Likely to Be Depressed and to Attempt Suicide," The Heritage Foundation, June 3, 2003, http://www.heritage.org/research/reports/2003/06/sexually-active-teenagers-are-more-likely-to-be-depressed?query=Sexually+Active+Teenagers+Are+More+Likely+to+Be+Depressed+and+to+Attempt+Suicide.

[30] Ibid.

[31] K. Aleisha Fetters, "What to Expect: Hospital Birth Costs," *Parents*, accessed January 31, 2015, http://www.parents.com/pregnancy/considering-baby/financing-family/birth-hospital-costs/.

[32] Melanie Hicken, "Average Cost of Raising a Child Hits $245,000," CNN.com, August, 18, 2014, http://money.cnn.com/2014/08/18/pf/child-cost/.

[33] The National Campaign to Prevent Teen and Unplanned Pregnancy, *Policy Brief: Preventing Teen Pregnancy is Critical to School Completion*, brief, July 2010, http://thenationalcampaign.org/sites/default/files/resource-primary-download/briefly_policybrief_school_completion.pdf.

[34] http://www.acog.org/-/media/Department-Publications/AdolescentFactsPregnancyAndSTDs.pdf?dmc=1&ts=20150311T1951287758

[35] Ibid.

[36] Ibid.

[37] Ibid.

[38] Saul D. Hoffman, *By the Numbers: The Public Cost of Teen Childbearing* (Washington, DC: The National Campaign to Prevent Teen and Unplanned Pregnancy, 2006), http://thenationalcampaign.org/sites/default/files/resource-primary-download/btn_national_report.pdf.

[39] The National Campaign to Prevent Teen and Unplanned Pregnancy, *Counting It Up: The Public Costs of Teen Childbearing: Key Data*, brief, December 2013, http://thenationalcampaign.org/sites/default/files/resource-primary-download/counting-it-up-key-data-2013-update.pdf.

[40] Centers for Disease Control and Prevention, *Incidence, Prevalence, and Cost of Sexually Transmitted Infections in the United States*, fact sheet, February 2013,

http://www.cdc.gov/std/stats/STI-Estimates-Fact-Sheet-Feb-2013.pdf.

[41]Robert Rector and Kirk A. Johnson, "Teenage Sexual Abstinence and Academic Achievement," The Heritage Foundation, October 27, 2005, http://www.heritage.org/research/reports/2005/10/teenage-sexual-abstinence-and-academic-achievement.

[42]Guttmacher Institute, *Facts on American Teens' Sources of Information about Sex*, fact sheet, February 2012, http://www.guttmacher.org/pubs/FB-Teen-Sex-Ed.html.

[43]Thomas Lickona, "Where Sex Education Went Wrong," *Educational Leadership*, March 1993, http://www.ascd.org/publications/educational-leadership/nov93/vol51/num03/Where-Sex-Education-Went-Wrong.aspx.

[44]"Discouraging Touch Comes with a Cost, Prof. Matt Hertenstein Writes in Providence Journal," Depauw University, March 23, 2009, http://www.depauw.edu/news-media/latest-news/details/23207/.

[45]Gary Chapman and Ross Campbell, *The 5 Love Languages of Children* (Chicago: Northfield Publishing, 2012), http://www.5lovelanguages.com/.

[46]1 Cor. 13:4-7 (New International Version).

[47]Jessica Bennett, "The Beta Marriage: How Millennials Approach "I Do,"' *Time*, July 25, 2014, http://time.com/3024606/millennials-marriage-sex-relationships-hook-ups/.

[48]D'Vera Cohn et al., "Barely Half of U.S. Adults Are Married—A Record Low," Pew Research Center, December 14, 2011, http://www.pewsocialtrends.org/2011/12/14/barely-half-of-u-s-adults-are-married-a-record-low/.

[49]"Millennials in Adulthood: Detached from Institutions, Networked with Friends," Pew Research Center, March 7, 2014, http://www.pewsocialtrends.org/2014/03/07/millennials-in-adulthood/.

[50]W. Bradford Wilcox, *Why Marriage Matters, Third Edition: Thirty Conclusions from the Social Sciences*, Third Edition (New York: Broadway Publications, 2011), http://www.psychpage.com/family/brwaitgalligher.html.

[51]"Dating Bill of Rights," The Clothesline Project, accessed January 31, 2015, http://www.clotheslineproject.org/Dating_Bill_of_Rights.htm.

[52]"Dating Rights," Washington State Office of the Attorney General, accessed March 3, 2015, http://www.atg.wa.gov/dating-rights.

[53]Tim Elmore, "The Marks of Maturity," *Psychology Today*, accessed January 31, 2015, https://www.psychologytoday.com/blog/artificial-maturity/201211/the-marks-maturity.

[54]Quote from Robert W. Blum, MD, PhD, in Siri Carpenter, "Teens' Risky Behavior Is about More Than Race and Family Resources," *Monitor on Psychology*, January 2001, http://www.apa.org/monitor/jan01/teenbehavior.aspx.

[55]Lauren Muhlheim, "Addressing Eating Disorders in Middle and High Schools," F.E.A.S.T., accessed January 31, 2015, http://www.feast-ed.org/Resources/ArticlesforFEAST/EatingDisordersinMiddleandHighSchools.aspx.

[56]Tamar Lewin, "Are These Parties for Real?" *The New York Times,* June 30, 2005, http://www.nytimes.com/2005/06/30/fashion/thursdaystyles/30rainbow.html?pagewanted=all.

[57]Elizabeth Boskey, "Is Oral Sex Safe Sex?" About.com, updated December 20, 2014, http://std.about.com/od/riskfactorsforstds/a/oralsexsafesex.htm.

[58]Centers for Disease Control and Prevention, *Oral Sex and HIV Risk*, fact sheet, updated May 21, 2014, http://www.cdc.gov/hiv/resources/factsheets/oralsex.htm.

[59]"Preven EC," Drugs.com, accessed March 5, 2015, http://www.drugs.com/mtm/preven-ec.html; Chris Kahlenborn, Joseph B. Stanford, and Walter L. Larimore, "Postfertilization Effect of Hormonal Emergency Contraception," *The Annals of Pharmacotherapy* 36 (2002):465, http://www.polycarp.org/postfertilization.pdf.

[60]"Plan B One-Step" accessed March 09, 2015, http://planbonestep.com/faqs.aspx, "ella" accessed March 09, 2015, http://www.ellanow.com/.

[61]Guttmacher Institute, *American Teens' Sexual and Reproductive Health*," fact sheet, May 2014, http://www.guttmacher.org/pubs/FB-ATSRH.html.

[62]Melanie Hicken, "Average Cost of Raising a Child Hits $245,000," CNN.com, August, 18, 2014, http://money.cnn.com/2014/08/18/pf/child-cost/.

[63]"Adoption Satisfaction," United States Department of Health and Human Services, accessed January 31, 2015, http://aspe.hhs.gov/hsp/09/NSAP/chartbook/chartbook.cfm?id=24.

[64]The National Campaign to Prevent Teen and Unplanned Pregnancy, *Fast Facts: Teen Pregnancy in the United States*, fact sheet, December 2013, http://thenationalcampaign.org/sites/default/files/resource-primary-download/fast_facts_-_teen_pregnancy_in_the_united_states_dec_2013.pdf.

[65]"Possible Physical Side Effects After Abortion," American Pregnancy Association, last updated February 2014, http://americanpregnancy.org/unplanned-pregnancy/abortion-side-effects/.

[66]"Lowit, A., Bhattacharya, S., & Bhattacharya, S. (2010). Obstetric performance following an induced abortion. Best Practice & Research in Clinical Obstetrics & Gynaecology, 24(5), 667-82. doi:10.1016/j.bpobgyn.2010.02.015. Swingle, H. M., Colaizy, T. T., Zimmerman, M. B., Morriss, F. H. (2009). Abortion and the risk of subsequent preterm birth: A systematic review with meta-analyses. *The Journal of Reproductive Medicine*, 54(2), 95-108.

[67]"Biology and epidemiology confirm the abortion-breast cancer link," accessed March 13, 2015. http://www.bcpinstitute.org/PDF/Complications-Chapter7.pdf, http://www.bcpinstitute.org/about.htm.

[68]"The American Cancer Society" Accessed March 07, 2015, http://www.cancer.org/cancer/breastcancer/moreinformation/is-abortion-linked-to-breast-cancer.

[69]C-c Hsieh et al., "Delivery of Premature Newborns and Maternal Breast Cancer Risk," *The Lancet* 353 (April 1999): Jose Russo et al., "Developmental, Cellular, and Molecular Basis of Human Breast Cancer," *Journal of the National Cancer Institute Monographs* 27 (2000):17-37.

[70]"Reproductive History and Breast Cancer Risk," National Cancer Institute, accessed February 14, 2011, http://www.cancer.gov/cancertopics/factsheet/Risk/pregnancy.

[71]"Biology and epidemiology confirm the abortion-breast cancer link," accessed March 13, 2015, http://www.bcpinstitute.org/PDF/Complications-Chapter7.pdf, http://www.bcpinstitute.org/about.htm. "Epidemiologic Studies: Induced

Abortion and Breast Cancer Risk," Breast Cancer Prevention Institute, 2013 http://www.bcpinstitute.org/epidemiology_studies_bcpi.htm.

[72]"National Cancer Institute and the National Institutes of Health" Accessed March 09, 2015, http://www.cancer.gov/cancertopics/factsheet/Risk/abortion-miscarriage.

[73]Priscilla K. Coleman, "Resolution of Unwanted Pregnancy during Adolescence through Abortion Versus Childbirth: Individual and Family Predictors and Psychological Consequences," *Journal of Youth and Adolescence* 35 (2006); Jesse R. Cougle, David C. Reardon, and Priscilla K. Coleman, "Generalized Anxiety Associated with Unintended Pregnancy: A Cohort Study of the 1995 National Survey of Family Growth," *Journal of Anxiety Disorders* 19 (2005); Anne Nordal Broen, Torbjörn Moum, Anne Sejersted Bödtker, Öivind Ekeberg, "Psychological Impact on Women of Miscarriage Versus Induced Abortion: A 2-Year Follow-up Study," *Psychosomatic Medicine* 66 (2004); Anne Nordal Broen, Torbjörn Moum, Anne Sejersted Bödtker, öivind Ekeberg, "The Course of Mental Health after Miscarriage and Induced Abortion: A Longitudinal, Five-Year Follow-Up Study," *BMC Medicine* 3 (2005):18.

[74]Amy R. Sobie and David C. Reardon, "Detrimental Effects of Adolescent Abortion," AfterAbortion.org, posted March 8, 2001, http://afterabortion.org/2001/detrimental-effects-of-adolescent-abortion/.

[75] John M. Thorp, Jr., Katherine E. Hartmann, and Elizabeth Shadigian, "Long-Term Physical and Psychological Health Consequences of Induced Abortion: Review of the Evidence," *Obstetrical & Gynecological Survey* 58, no. 1 (January 2003); "Position Statement on Women's Mental Health in Relation to Induced Abortion," Royal College of Psychiatrists, March 14, 2008, http://bjp.rcpsych.org/content/199/3/180.

[76]Coleman, P.K., Coyle, C., Rue, V. (2010). Late-term elective abortion and susceptibility to posttraumatic stress symptoms. Journal of Pregnancy,Retrieved on July 20, 2014 from http://dx.doi.org/10.1155/2010/130519.

[77]P.K. Coleman, V.M. Rue, and C.T. Coyle, "Induced Abortion and Intimate Relationship Quality in the Chicago Health and Social Life Survey," *Public Health* 123, no. 4 (April 2009).

[78]"The Rights of Unmarried Fathers," Child Welfare Information Gateway, accessed May 20, 2014, https:

//www.childwelfare.gov/systemwide/laws_policies/statutes/putative.cfm.

[79] Bonnie Rochman, "The Results Are In: First National Study of Teen Masturbation," *Time*, August 11, 2011, http://healthland.time.com/2011/08/11/boys-masturbate-more-than-girls-seriously/.

[80] Cynthia L. Robbins et al., "Prevalence, Frequency, and Associations of Masturbation with Partnered Sexual Behaviors among US Adolescents," *Archives of Pediatrics & Adolescent Medicine* 165 no. 12 (2011), accessed January 31, 2015, http://archpedi.ama-assn.org/cgi/content/abstract/archpediatrics.2011.142.

[81] Peggy J. Kleinplatz, *New Directions in Sex Therapy: Innovations and Alternatives* (New York: Routledge, 2012), 58.

[82] Mike Celizic, "Her Teen Committed Suicide Over 'Sexting'," NBC *Today*, March 6, 2009, http://www.today.com/id/29546030/ns/today-parenting_and_family/t/her-teen-committed-suicide-over-sexting/\#.U6A1TvldXTo.

[83] "Evanston Baseball 'Sexting': High School Baseball Team Pulled From Playoffs Over Pic Scandal," *Huffington Post Chicago*, May 24, 2013, http://www.huffingtonpost.com/2013/05/24/evanston-baseball-sexting_n_3332752.html.

[84] "2012 Sexting Legislation," National Conference of State Legislatures, accessed June 17, 2014, http://www.ncsl.org/research/telecommunications-and-information-technology/sexting-legislation-2012.aspx.

[85] Scott Daugherty, "Suffolk Boy, 13, Charged in Alleged 'Sextortion' Case," PilotOnline.com, May 28, 2014, http://hamptonroads.com/2014/05/suffolk-boy-13-charged-alleged-sextortion-case.

[86] "'It's Rape': Sayreville High School Players Face Charges of Abusive Hazing," BBC News, last updated October 22, 2014, http://www.bbc.com/news/blogs-echochambers-29716923.

[87] "Former Teacher Charged with Sexually Assaulting Student," NBCDFW.com, published January 15, 2015, http://www.nbcdfw.com/news/local/Former-Teacher-Charged-With-Sexually-Assaulting-Student-288691921.html.

[88] "The Penn State Scandal," CBS.com, accessed January 31, 2015,

http://www.cbsnews.com/feature/the-penn-state-scandal/.

[89] "Sexual Abuse Statistics," Teen Help, accessed January 31, 2015, http://www.teenhelp.com/teen-abuse/sexual-abuse-stats.html.

[90] "Teenage Drinking: Understanding the Dangers and Talking to Your Child," Helpguide.org, accessed March 6, 2015, http://www.helpguide.org/harvard/the-dangers-of-teenage-drinking.htm.

[91] Ibid.

[92] National Center for HIV/AIDS, Viral Hepatitis, STD, and TB Prevention, *Trends in the Prevalence of Alcohol Use: National YRBS: 1991-2011*, accessed January 31, 2015, http://www.cdc.gov/healthyyouth/yrbs/pdf/us_alcohol_trend_yrbs.pdf. For additional details and breakdown of statistics by gender and by states, see the Alcohol and Other Drug Use links at http://apps.nccd.cdc.gov/youthonline/App/QuestionsOrLocations.aspx?CategoryID=3. On binge drinking and young women, see http://www.cdc.gov/alcohol/fact-sheets/underage-drinking.htm.

[93] Scott Stevens, "Teen Drinking under Parent's Eye Not Harmless: Damages Brain, Encourages Trouble," *Alchologist.com* (blog), October 15, 2014, http://alcoholauthor.blogspot.com/2014/10/teen-drinking-under-parents-eye-not.html.

[94] "Date Rape Drugs," Brown University, accessed January 31, 2015, http://www.brown.edu/Student_Services/Health_Services/Health_Education/sexual_assault_\&_dating_violence/date_rape_drugs.php.

[95] https://rainn.org/get-information/types-of-sexual-assault/drug-facilitated-assault, http://www.idph.state.il.us/about/womenshealth/factsheets/date.htm.

[96] "Teenage Drinking: Understanding the Dangers and Talking to Your Child," Helpguide.org, accessed March 6, 2015, http://www.helpguide.org/harvard/the-dangers-of-teenage-drinking.htm.

[97] "Growing Support for Gay Marriage: Changed Minds and Changing Demographics," Pew Research Center, March, 20, 2013, http://www.people-press.org/2013/03/20/growing-support-for-gay-marriage-changed-minds-and-changing-demographics/.

[98] Many of the guidelines offered in this "Where to Begin?" section were adapted with permission from the following source: John Pavlovitz, "10 Things Christian Parents Can Do When Their Kids Come Out," *John Pavlovitz: Stuff That Needs to Be Said* (blog), accessed March 6, 2015, http://johnpavlovitz.com/2015/01/20/10-things-christian-parents-can-do-when-their-kids-come-out/.

ACKNOWLEDGMENTS

Thanks to family, friends, and co-laborers for their confidence and continuous encouragement to write: Kelli Huntley, Courtney Harelston Johnson, Mimi Harris, The Beacon Team, Jen Wisler, Lynn Bouchillon, Ally Richey, Lori Reichart, Trey Massey, Greg Stipe, Jeff Jacobson, Beth Huegli, Jeff Richardson, Robin Shultz, Julie Rayburn, Janee Garrett, Steve Stroup, and KC Steury.

Thanks to the following individuals for lending me their expertise, talent, and insights and aiding me in this writing project: Natalie Floyd, Larry Whittington, Michael Moellering, Brian Beam, Beth Jusino, Kathy Burge, Jenn Reese, Brad Sargent, Matt Jacobson, Sharon Heggeland, Heidi Mitchell, Abby Johnson, Gayle Bucher, and Andy Stanley.

Thanks to all of the parents who have attended my parent workshops over the last fifteen years. Your consistent comment "you should write a book" finally paid off.

A special thanks to all the young girls and families who allowed me to share their personal stories. My hope, my prayer, is that the nights of tears have given way to days of laughter and rejoicing.

ABOUT THE AUTHOR

Talli Moellering is a wife, a mom, a speaker, and a sexual risk avoidance specialist with fifteen years of experience in the field of sexual health. In 2012 she launched a Prevention Initiative and since then has presented her Pure Sexual Freedom model to thousands of middle- and high-school students and their parents across the United States. In addition, she has also trained public school educators to deliver the standard sex education curriculum.

Talli is the executive director of a women's medical clinic in the Atlanta area that specializes in sexual health and unplanned pregnancies, which gives her the daily opportunity to work directly with sexually active teens and their families. Prior to this, Talli co-founded and was the executive director of True Life Choices, a non-profit organization in Indiana. She is a post-abortion recovery specialist, has a Crisis Pregnancy Coach certification through the American Association of Christian Counselors (AACC), and a bachelor's degree in business administration.

Talli and her husband David have been married for twenty-five years and are the parents of three high school and college-age daughters, who regularly provide them with real-life scenarios that added to Talli's practical, realistic teaching methods.

Visit Talli online at www.tallitalk.com or www.tlcconsultantsinc.com

CPSIA information can be obtained at www.ICGtesting.com
Printed in the USA
LVOW11s1634280515

440292LV00003B/560/P